Descendants of
John Michael Kreider
of
Montgomery County, Pennsylvania

— CRIDER FAMILIES OF VIRGINIA, KENTUCKY AND TENNESSEE —

Rebecca L. Blackwell

HERITAGE BOOKS
2007

HERITAGE BOOKS

AN IMPRINT OF HERITAGE BOOKS, INC.

Books, CDs, and more—Worldwide

For our listing of thousands of titles see our website
at
www.HeritageBooks.com

Published 2007 by
HERITAGE BOOKS, INC.
Publishing Division
65 East Main Street
Westminster, Maryland 21157-5026

International Standard Book Number: 978-0-7884-1091-8

Dedication

This book is dedicated
To my mother,
Christine Joyce Jones,
And to her mother,
My grandmother,
Anita Crider.

Descendants of John Michael Kreider

Table of Contents

Acknowledgements

*I wish to thank the following researchers and relatives
for their kind contributions to this book. In particular,
I wish to thank Bob Oliver and The Montgomery County
Pennsylvania Historical Society for locating Michael Kreider.*

(in alphabetical order)

E.W. Crider
Sante Fe, New Mexico

Carl and Lorene Dunbar
El Paso, Texas

Clyde B. East
Agoura, California

Henrietta Edwards
Albuquerque, New Mexico

Virginia King
Maryville, Tennessee

Robert Oliver
Nixa, Missouri

Frank Rice, Jr.
Diana, Texas

Christine J. Roe
Dayton, Ohio

Michael Kreider's signature on the passenger list of the ship "Samuel", 1732 (see page 1).

Michael Kreider's signature on a road petition, March 6, 1758 (see page 2).

Crider Families of Virginia, Kentucky and Tennessee

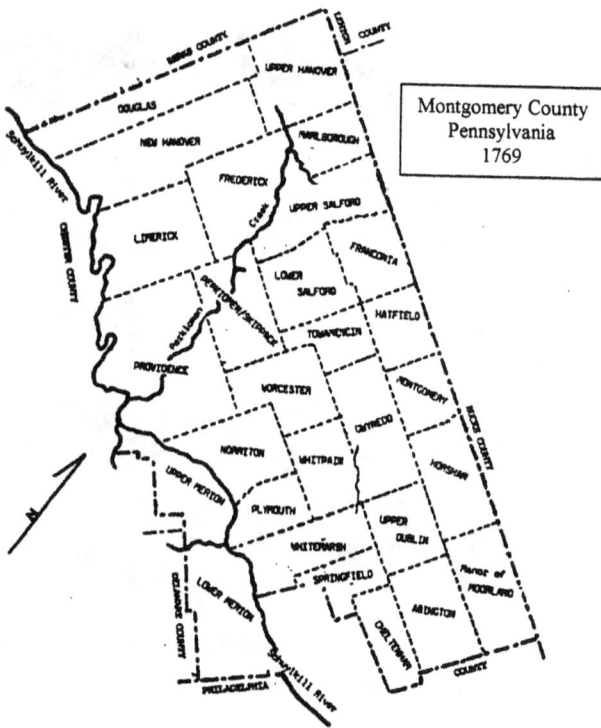

Montgomery County
Pennsylvania
1769

Montgomery County, Pennsylvania,
was formed from Philadelphia County in 1784.

Descendants of John Michael Kreider
of Montgomery County, Pennsylvania

♦ **Crider Families of Virginia, Kentucky and Tennessee** ♦

FIRST GENERATION

1. JOHN MICHAEL1 KREIDER was born about 1712 in Germany, and died in July, 1761, in Hatfield Township, Philadelphia Co., Pennsylvania.

Michael Kreider, age 20, arrived in Philadelphia on August 11, 1732 aboard the ship "Samuel" from Rotterdam. He signed his name in longhand on the ship's register, indicating he was an educated man. As none of the other 268 passengers bore the name Kreider, we assume Michael made the journey alone.

On September 25, 1732, on the ship "Loyal Judith" of London, also from Holland, Peter (45) and Johannes (37) Kreider arrived in Philadelphia. They settled near Michael in Perkiomen/Skippack Township, Philadelphia County, indicating they were possibly relatives (see note). Emigration records indicate that Michael was from the Palatine Region of Germany. It is suspected that his ancestry may have been Swiss, whether or not he was truly born in Germany. Most Kreider families in Pennsylvania have been traced back to Switzerland during the Reformation. From there, many families settled in Germany temporarily before immigrating to America.

Michael became a blacksmith and the owner of a grist mill in Hatfield Township, Philadelphia County (later Montgomery Co.), near the Bucks County line. On March 7, 1734, he signed a road petition in Hanover Township; his signature matches that shown on the ship's register.

In 1743 a Michael Kreider of Philadelphia County "scrupled to take the Oath" of citizenship, indicating he may have been a Mennonite. This is assumed to be our Michael as no other man by that name was living in Philadelphia County at the time. Also, other Philadelphia County neighbors were given citizenship on that date (i.e. Jacob Wierman, below). Given that our Michael did not settle in the strongly Mennonite communities in Lancaster and Lebanon Counties, and he later attended Reformed and Lutheran churches, we may assume that our Michael either was not a Mennonite (perhaps he just got in line with his Mennonite friends) or he did not retain his faith. Other Kreider families lived in the city of Philadelphia who were also of the Reformed faith (the Reformed church is basically Presbyterian in structure and belief, although it was founded in Switzerland).

In 1748 Michael Kreider bought 73 acres of land in Hatfield Township from Jacob Wierman, a German Mennonite. This land was bounded by the properties of Rudolph Lapp, the late Richard Davis, David Evans, Henry Shooter and Michael Wierman. Two years later, Michael purchased another tract of 21 acres, as well as one acre from neighbor Rudolph Lapp.

On Jan. 16, 1753, Michael purchased 100 acres of land in Upper Salford Township from Frederick Hertzog.

September 15, 1753, Michael Krauter attended the Lord's Supper at Indian Field Lutheran Church in Franconia Township. On October 14, 1753, two servants of Michael Krauter named Barbara Gerhardt and Maria Barbara Conrad attended Confession at the same church. Apparently, Michael was already wealthy enough to employ, not one, but two servants in his home.

March 6, 1758, "The Honorable Justices of the Court of Quarter Sessions, Held at Philadelphia..." appointed "a judicious set of men to view and lay out a Road to begin in the Bucks County line near John

Benner's Plantation, Thence by the Presbyterian Meeting House (the Indian Creek Reformed Church Michael attended), and the Lutheran Church to Michael Croyder's Grist Mill." Michael Kreider signed this paper as one of the members of the jury appointed to lay out the road. *The Bulletin of the Historical Society of Montgomery County, Vol. 8, No.3* (Oct 83), mentions the laying of this road and questions..."Why they wanted to get to Croyder's Mill up on the Ridge Valley Creek remains a mystery--perhaps Moyer at his mill was not giving them good service! Be that as it may, the Court graciously agreed to lay out such a road, and on the 9th and 10th of May it was surveyed and marked."

However, at the Quarter Sessions held June 5, 1758, a petition was filed by "the Subscribers and Inhabitants of Franconia and Salford Townships," complaining that the road was laid out through their "plantations and woodlands," and "will be of very little public use But Chiefly for the Convenience of One of a few private persons." Could they have been referring to Michael Kreider? They requested another jury be appointed to review the laying of the road. Accordingly, some changes were made to the road, running along the county line for a longer distance to avoid cutting through Benner and Hunsberger's land.

No marriage record has been found to date, but we know Michael's wife was Catherine for she is mentioned in the baptismal records for several of their children. Their youngest child, David, was baptized along with their grandchild, John Jacob, son of John and Mary Barbara Krider. Catherine must have been in her early 40's when David was born.

"Michael Kreider, Blacksmith" wrote his will July 7, 1761, in Hatfield Township. He mentions wife Catherine, children John, Jacob, Abraham, Daniel, Catherine, Magdelena and David. "Loving wife, Catherine" received "our Matrimonial bed and Furniture..Cows and one third part of my personal Estate." "Oldest son, John, all that one hundred acres of Land situated in Upper Salford Township which I bought of Frederick Hertzog...together with all...the improvements Grist Mill and Saw Mill on the said 100 acres of land. In return, John was to pay the sum of 200 pounds to "all my other children." Michael specified exactly what amount was to be paid on each of several dates for nine years following his death, "...without any Interest provided he payeth his said payments at the hereby fixed times." Son Abraham received "all that plantation or Tract of Land Conveyed to me in two Parcels by Jacob Wierman situated in Hatfield aforesaid containing one hundred acres of Land, by the same more or less...after he is arrived at the age of twenty one years." When Abraham acquired his property, he was to pay the sum of 105 pounds to the younger children in a similar manner to that set up for John. Son Daniel was bequeathed, "all that Part of Tract of Land Situated in Upper Salford adjoining to the Land hereby granted to my son John Containing seventy four acres of land, be it more or less, twenty four which were conveyed to me by Frederick Hertzog and fifty acres whereof warranted to me by the Honourable Proprietor..after he is arrived at the age of 21 years." He was also to pay the "arrears due" the Proprietor. Son Jacob, which is absconded from me if he happens to return again (is bequeathed) the sum of fifty pounds." Daughters Catherine and Magdelena were willed 100 pounds each to be received.."after they have attained the age of 18 years." "Youngest child, David" was also to receive 100 pounds to be "paid to him at his lawful age." He willed that his wife was to "Continue the Housekeeping on the Improvement whereon I now Dwell with the Children under age as long as she pleaseth but if she happened to marry again or in case of her Death the said Improvements and all the Stock and Household goods shall be sold by Publick Sale and moneys gott by said Sale Shall be Divided..." Good citizen Michael also bequeathed money to the "Poor of the Province." The will was proven August 1, 1761, indicating that he died in the month of July at the age of 49.

Note: Peter and John Kreider often appear in Philadelphia County and Montgomery County records as Kider or Kiter. They both lived in Skippack/Perkiomen Townships, southeast of Upper Salford. Peter appears in the 1769 Tax Assessments as a miller, owning a grist mill (like Michael and two of his sons), 180 acres, 3 horses and 2 cattle (Peter was old enough to be Michael's father, but no evidence has been found to support a relationship). John was listed as a tavern keeper with 100 acres, 3 horses, and 5 cattle. Apparently both prospered in their new country and were probably not destitute upon their arrival. Peter and John are listed on the Salford Store Ledger in Upper Salford Township between the years 1766 and 1774, along with John and Daniel Krider, sons of Michael. There is an entry in the store ledger for Peter Becker who is noted as being "the taylor (tailor) at Peter Kider's." This indicates that Peter was probably having a new set of clothes made for himself and/or his family. A Peter Kider appears as a Private in the 3rd Company of Capt. Barnet Hains of the Lower Dist. of Skippack, Philadelphia County Militia, 1780 (*PA Archives*, 3rd Series, Vol. 15). This appears to be a younger Peter as the man who arrived in 1732 at the age of 45 would have been 93 years old! John Crator (sic) appears as a Private First Class in the 5th Company of Capt. John Harples of the Upper District of Skippack; again this must be a descendant of the original John of the same township (Ibid.). A reference has been found to the marriage of Johan Wilhelm Kreuter, son of Johan Philip Kreuter and dec'd wife Elisabeth, in Skippack Township, 1756. This Johan Sr. must be the same person as John of Skippack who arrived in 1732. His son, known as William Kreider, and his wife, Catherine, appear in the church records of Indian Field Lutheran Church along with Michael Kreider and wife Catherine.

A possibility as to the parents of Michael: a Michael Kreider married Anna Maria Schwartzin July 30, 1711, at the Evangelisch-Lutherische, Bad Duerkheim, Pfalz, Bavaria. This date would coincide with Michael's birth in 1712. Sons often were given their father's names, and many of Michael's descendants were named Maria. Also, the religious affiliation is the same as Michael's. (*Extracted Marriage Records*, Microfilm Batch M997432, 1640-1716, Call number 488270.)

2.   i.   JOHN2 KRIDER, b. Abt.. 1735, Hatfield Township, Philadelphia Co., Pennsylvania; d. Aft. 1784.

       ii.   JOHN JACOB KRIDER, b. 1740, Hatfield Township, Philadelphia Co., Pennsylvania.

John Jacob Krauter (sic), son of Michael, age 15 years, was confirmed Mar. 30, 1755, by Rev. Frederick Schultz at the Indian Field Lutheran Church, Franconia Township, Philadelphia (now Montgomery) County, Pennsylvania (LDS Microfilm)

Jacob is mentioned in his father's will as "having absconded from me". He was left 50 pounds in the event he returned to the family after his father's death. Nothing further is known about his life.

A Jacob Krider joined the Philadelphia City Militia on Oct. 25, 1777.

A daughter of Jacob and Elisabeth Kreiter, Catharina, was born Oct. 16, 1782, and baptized May 18, 1783, at the New Hanover Lutheran Church in Montgomery County The sponsors were Daniel Kreiter and Elisabeth Dotterer (*Pennsylvania German Church Records*, Vol. 1) Jacob's brother, John, did attend this church after his move to New Hanover Township. However, this could also be John Jacob Krider, son of John and Barbara, and the sponsor, Daniel, his younger brother.

This may be the Jacob Crator who wrote his will in Montgomery County, Dec. 23, 1820, and probated Nov. 28, 1822 (Book 6, p. 79). He left a wife, Catherine, and children John, Peter, and Catherine. The Executors were Martin Funk and Christian Stegnor. The Witnesses were Isaac Morris and Peter Benner (the Benners were numerous in Upper Salford and Marlborough Townships). It may be impossible to determine Jacob's identity.

3.   iii.   ABRAHAM KRIDER, b. 1742, Hatfield Township, Philadelphia
                Co., Pennsylvania; d. Aft. 1790, Pennsylvania.
4.   iv.   DANIEL KRIDER, b. 1744, Hatfield Township, Philadelphia
                Co., Pennsylvania; d. 1836, Toshes, Pittsylvania Co., Virginia.
5.   v.   CATHERINE KRIDER, b. April 27, 1749, Hatfield Township,
                Philadelphia Co., Pennsylvania. Christened: June 16, 1749,
                Augustus Church, New Providence, Philadelphia Co.,
                Pennsylvania.

                Catherine was baptized "Catherina" at the Evangelical
                Lutheran Augustus Church at Trappe, New Providence,
                Montgomery (then Philadelphia) County, Pennsylvania. The
                sponsors were her parents, Michael and Catherina, "in Indian
                Field" (*Pennsylvania German Church Records*, Vol. 1, p.
                379).

        vi.   MAGDELENA KRIDER, b. August 08, 1754, Hatfield
                Township, Philadelphia Co., Pennsylvania. Christened:
                September 16, 1754, Indian Field Church, Franconia
                Township, Philadelphia Co., Pennsylvania

                Magdelena, daughter of Michael Krauter and wife Catharine,
                was baptized by Rev. Frederick Schultz at the Indian Field
                Lutheran Church, Franconia Township, Philadelphia (now
                Montgomery) County, Pennsylvania. The witnesses were John
                Neiss (Nice) and wife Catharine

        ii.   DAVID KRIDER, b. January 14, 1758, Hatfield Township,
                Philadelphia Co., Pennsylvania. Christened: November 16,
                1760, Tohickon Reformed Church., Bedminster Township,
                Bucks Co., Pennsylvania.

                "David Kreuter, son of Michael Kreuter and Catharine, was
                baptized on the same day as his nephew, John Jacob, son of
                John and Mary Barbara Krider, at the Tohickon Reformed
                Church, Bedminster Township, Bucks County, Pennsylvania
                (*Pennsylvania German Church Records*, Vol. 3, p. 110).

7

SECOND GENERATION

2. JOHN2 KRIDER *(JOHN MICHAEL1 KREIDER)* was born Abt.. 1735 in Hatfield Township, Philadelphia Co., Pennsylvania, and died Aft. 1784.

Although the surname Krider was spelled in a variety of ways, the spelling shown here seems to be the most common during John's generation.

On June 24, 1752, "Johann Kreuter, aged 17 years, son of Michael Kreuter," was confirmed at the Lutheran Congregation of Old Goshenhoppen in Upper Salford, Philadelphia County (now Montgomery Co.). This would indicate that John was born about 1735 ("Translation of the Records of the Lutheran Congregation at Old Goshenhoppen," *The Perkiomen Region*, Vol. 1, No. 3, p. 78).

May 19, 1755, John Krauter attended Confession at Indian Field Lutheran Church in Franconia Township. His father attended the same church in 1753.

John Krider inherited the 100 acres in Upper Salford Township that his father purchased from Frederick Hertzog along with the grist mill and saw mill on that land. In return, John was to pay a set sum each year to the younger siblings for the nine years following his father's death.

John appeared in the 1769 Proprietary Tax List as living in Upper Salford, owning the same 100 acres and a forge, 4 horses, 3 cows and two sheep. In 1774 he appears in Marlborough Township owning only 2 horses and 2 cows; although he does not appear in the tax list for Upper Salford, he apparently still owned the forge and land in that township. In the 1779 Effective Supply Tax lists he appears in Upper Salford with a valuation of 122 pounds tax. He paid 32 pounds state tax in the same year, also in Upper Salford. John does not appear in the tax lists after 1779 (*PA Archives*, 3rd Series, Vol. 14, 15 and 16).

A deed recorded July 28, 1770, shows that the Proprietors granted John Cryder (Krider) and his wife, Mary Barbara, 72 acres comprising "...the Forge Tract in Upper Salford Township on the east bank of the Perkiomen..." This same deed, indentured in 1779, identifies the property further as being, "Together with the Forge for making of Bar Iron thereon erected and built..." (Deed Book No.8, p.668-669, Court House, Norristown, PA).

The ledger for Salford Store for the years 1766 to 1774 shows John Krider's account beginning Jan. 20, 1767, indicating the forge was in existence at that time. Storekeeper Michael Croll transported some of John Krider's iron to Philadelphia July 21,1768, according to the entry for that date. As further proof, the forge is listed in the 1769 assessments for Upper Salford, the earliest tax records available.

A notice in "Staatsbote", a German language newspaper published in Philadelphia, dated November 19, 1776, states: "Johannes Kreiter offers for sale a furnace in Upper Salford Township (Montgomery County), with 370 acres" (*Genealogical Data Related to German Settlers of Pennsylvania and Adjacent Territory From Advertisements in German Newspapers Published in Philadelphia and Germantown, 1743-1800*).

Although records are not complete during the War years, John apparently did not sell the forge in 1776 because he is assessed for the property in 1779. On June 24,1779 John Krider and wife, Mary Barbara, granted 72 acres of land, forge and dwelling to William Bird of Reading, Pennsylvania. Bird sold the property Oct. 9, 1779, to John Patton of Berks County and Samuel Moore of Reading, PA, for 20,000 pounds (the inflated price due to the War economy).

John Krider appears on a list of Non-Associators of the Township of Limerick, 1779 (*PA Archives*, 2nd Series, Vol. 14, p. 24). However, a note at the head of the lists indicates that the original lists were probably mislabeled as many of those listed served in the Revolutionary War. John may be the John Krider who served as a Private in Capt. Honey's Company of the Northern District of the City Guards, Philadelphia City Militia. This will be investigated further.

John apparently moved to Limerick Township after he sold his property in Upper Salford. He attended services at the New Hanover Lutheran Church in New Hanover Township, just north of Limerick. Four of his children were confirmed there in 1782 and 1784 (*Pennsylvania German Church Records*, Vol. 2).

John Krider has not been located in the 1790 census of Pennsylvania; he may have moved his family elsewhere, as his widow is also not listed.

♥ John married MARIA BARBARA Bef. 1758 in Philadelphia Co., Pennsylvania.

Children of JOHN KRIDER and MARIA BARBARA are:

    i.   JOHN JACOB3 KRIDER, b. August 1, 1758, Philadelphia Co., Pennsylvania. Christened: November 16, 1760, Tohickon Reformed Church, Bedminster Township, Bucks Co., Pennsylvania

        John Jacob was baptized the same day as his uncle, David. His parents were listed as John Kreuter and wife Barbara. The sponsor was Jacob Leydy (*Pennsylvania German Church Records*, Vol. 3, p. 110).

    ii. DANIEL KRIDER, b. 1760, Philadelphia Co., Pennsylvania.

Daniel Kreiter, son of Johann Kreiter, was confirmed at New Hanover Lutheran Church on Saturday, May 18, 1782. His age was given as 22 years (*Pennsylvania German Church Records*, Vol. 2, p. 318).

iii. ELIZABETH KRIDER, b. Abt.. 1764, Philadelphia Co., Pennsylvania. Married FREDERICK MEISHEIMER, New Hanover Township, Montgomery Co., Pennsylvania.

Elizabeth Krider, age not given, was confirmed before the congregation of the New Hanover Lutheran Church on the Saturday before Pentecost, May 18, 1782. Also confirmed on that date was her brother, Daniel, age 22. Her father is listed as Johann Kreiter (*Pennsylvania German Church Records*, Vol. 2, p. 318).

iv. ANNA BARBARA KRIDER, b. July 26, 1767, Upper Salford, Philadelphia Co., Pennsylvania. Christened: 1767, Old Goshenhoppen, Upper Salford, Philadelphia Co., Pennsylvania

Anna Barbara was baptized in the Lutheran Congregation at Old Goshenhoppen Church, Upper Salford Township, in what is now Montgomery County. Her parents are listed as Johannes Kreuter and wife Maria Barbara; the Sponsors were Anna Barbara Doetter and Johann Heister, both single (*The Perkiomen Region*, Vol. 2 No. 3, p. 57).

Anna Barbara was confirmed and received her first communion Whit Sunday, May 29, 1784 at the New Hanover Lutheran Church, New Hanover Township, Montgomery County. She was sixteen years old, daughter of Johannes Kreiter (*Pennsylvania German Church Records*, Vol. 2, p. 320).

v. MAGDELENA KRIDER, b. 1770, Philadelphia Co., Pennsylvania.

Magdelena Kreiter, daughter of Johannes Kreiter, was confirmed with her older sister, Anna Barbara, on Whit

Sunday, May 29, 1784, at New Hanover Lutheran Church, New Hanover Township, Montgomery County, Pennsylvania. She was 14 years old (*Pennsylvania German Church Records*, Vol. 2, p. 320).

vi. CATHARINA KRIDER, b. September 1772, Philadelphia Co., Pennsylvania; d. October 1775, Old Goshenhoppen, Upper Salford, Philadelphia Co., Pennsylvania. Buried: October 12, 1775, Old Goshenhoppen, Upper Salford, Philadelphia Co., Pennsylvania

According to the Church Records of Old Goshenhoppen Lutheran Church, Upper Salford Township, Catharina, daughter of John Kreuther, was buried Oct. 12, 1775, aged 3 years "less six weeks" (LDS Microfilm of the original records).

3. ABRAHAM2 KRIDER *(JOHN MICHAEL1 KREIDER)* was born in 1742 in Hatfield Township, Philadelphia Co., Pennsylvania, and died Aft. 1790 in Pennsylvania.

Abraham Kreiter (sic), son of Michael Kreiter, age 15, was confirmed April 10, 1757 by Rev. John Joseph Roth at Indian Field Lutheran Church, Franconia Township, Philadelphia (now Montgomery) County, Pennsylvania (LDS Microfilm).

Abraham Krider inherited 95 acres of land in Upper Salford Township from his father in 1761. His father stated that he was underage; he would have been 19 years old, according to his confirmation four years earlier.

Like his father and brothers John and Daniel, Abraham was a blacksmith by trade. He sold the land he inherited Dec. 7, 1763, to Jacob Cline (Klein), but he continued to live in Upper Salford Township as shown by the tax lists. In the 1769 Proprietary Tax (the first year of its existence) of Philadelphia County, Abraham owned no land but was listed with one horse and two cows. He also appears in the Tax Lists of 1774 (Provincial Tax), 1779 (Supply Tax and State Tax) and 1780 (Supply Tax). It appears he was not as well-off as his brothers; his fortunes were quite meager until 1780 when his property was valued at 250 pounds. In the 1781 Supply Tax list, Abraham is shown owning property valued at only 68 pounds and is listed as a "laborer". He does not appear in the 1783 lists in Upper Salford. In the first census of 1790, Abraham appears in Montgomery County (which was formed from part of Philadelphia Co. in 1784) with four white souls, one dwelling, and four other buildings (*PA Archives*, 3rd Series, Vol. 14, 15 and 16).

Abraham appears in a list of Non-Associators of Philadelphia County (later Montgomery County) for the years 1778-1779 (*PA Archives*, 2nd Series, Vol. 14, p.34). However, a note at the head of this list indicates the original was probably mislabeled as several men on the list were known to have served in the Revolutionary War, and it is actually an assessment list. Abraham Krider of Upper Salford Township served as a Private, 3rd Class, in the 7th Company of Capt. Nevel, 5th District of Philadelphia County Militia under Colonel Daniel Hiester, 1780 (*PA Archives*, 6th Series, Vol. 1, p.833).

In the 1790 census of Montgomery County, Abraham Crider is shown with 4 males 16 and over including himself, one male under 16, and four females including his wife. This would indicate he probably had four sons and three daughters.

♥ Abraham married ANNA ELIZABETH ERHARD May 13, 1762 in Indian Field Church, Franconia Township, Philadelphia Co., Pennsylvania.

The marriage record of Abraham Kreuter and Elizabeth Erhard was recorded May 13, 1762, at Indian Field Lutheran Church (see above). The minister was Rev. Frederick Shultz (LDS Microfilm).

Children of ABRAHAM KRIDER and ANNA ERHARD are:

i. JOHN3 KRIDER, b. November 9, 1767, Philadelphia Co., Pennsylvania. Christened: Indian Field Lutheran Church, Franconia Township, Philadelphia Co., Pennsylvania.

John, son of Abraham Kreiter, was baptized by Rev. Frederick Schultz at the Indian Field Lutheran Church, Franconia Township, Philadelphia (now Montgomery) County, Pennsylvania. The sponsor was Anthony Lichtel (LDS Microfilm).

ii. ANNA BARBARA KRIDER, b. July 25, 1770, Upper Salford, Philadelphia Co., Pennsylvania; d. February 6, 1773, Old Goshenhoppen, Upper Salford, Philadelphia Co., Pennsylvania. Christened: May 19, 1771, Old Goshenhoppen, Upper Salford, Philadelphia Co., Pennsylvania. Buried: February 19, 1773, Old Goshenhoppen, Upper Salford, Philadelphia Co., Pennsylvania

Anna Barbara was baptized in the Lutheran Congregation of Old Goshenhoppen Church at Upper Salford Township in what is now Montgomery County. Parents were listed as Abraham Creuter and wife Anna Elisabeth. The Sponsors were Philip Fisher and Margaretha Hobias, both single (*The Perkiomen Region*, Vol. 2, No. 3, p. 57).

In the Church Records of Old Goshenhoppen Lutheran Church, Upper Salford, Anna Barbara, daughter of Abraham Kreuther, was buried Feb. 19, 1773. When she died she was, "...age 3 years, 6 months, 12 days" (LDS Microfilm of the original records).

iii. MARIA EVA KRIDER, b. March 17, 1776, Philadelphia Co., Pennsylvania. Christened: April 8, 1776, Indian Field Lutheran Church, Franconia Township, Philadelphia Co., Pennsylvania.

15

Maria Eva was baptized at the Indian Field Lutheran Church
in Franconia Township, Philadelphia (now Montgomery)
County, Pennsylvania. Her parents were listed as Abraham
Kreuther and Anna Elisabeth. The Sponsors were George
Wald and wife Maria Eva (LDS Microfilm).

iv. MAGDELENA KRIDER, b. September 12, 1779, Philadelphia
Co., Pennsylvania. Christened: January 1, 1780, Indian Field
Lutheran Church, Franconia Township, Philadelphia Co.,
Pennsylvania.

Magdelena was baptized in the Indian Field Lutheran Church
in Franconia Township, Philadelphia County (now
Montgomery County), Pennsylvania. Her parents were listed as
Abraham Kreuther and Anna Elisabeth. The Sponsors were
Ludwig Pilger and wife Magdelena (LDS Microfilm).

4. DANIEL2 KRIDER *(JOHN MICHAEL1 KREIDER)* was born in 1744 in
Hatfield Township, Philadelphia Co., Pennsylvania, and died in 1836 in
Toshes, Pittsylvania Co., Virginia.

Daniel's birthdate was given as 1744 by schoolteacher Winston Dalton
in his Register. Dalton kept records of important dates concerning his
neighbors in Pittsylvania County. This date is not proven but it is
reasonable as Daniel was under 21 years of age when his father wrote
his will in 1761. Also, he was younger, it seems, than his brother
Abraham, who was born in 1742 according to his confirmation. Daniel
is the only child of Michael and Catherine whose baptism or
confirmation has not been found.

Michael Kreider left to his son Daniel 74 acres of land adjoining the
tract bequeathed to his brother John, containing 24 acres purchased
from Jacob Wierman and 50 acres warranted by the Proprietor. It
appears that the 24 acres were in Upper Salford and the remainder in

Marlborough Township, directly north. Marlborough was formed in 1745 from the northeastern portion of Upper Salford. Daniel appears in tax lists for both townships, although not simultaneously.

In the first Proprietary Tax of Philadelphia County (1769), Daniel appears in Upper Salford, owning only 25 acres of land, one horse and two cows. In 1774 he appears in Marlborough with 20 (?) acres and two cows. Again, he is in Marlborough in 1779 (State Tax), 1780 (Supply Tax) with a valuation of 1,450 pounds, and 1783 (Federal Tax) with 62 acres, 2 horses, 2 cows and 3 sheep. Also in 1783 Daniel is shown as renting 39 acres in Upper Salford from the estate of Christian Martin. In the 1785 tax assessments in Marlborough Township, Daniel Krider is shown as owning 62 acres and dwelling, 1 small hammer, 2 horses, 1 cow and 1 hemp mill, total valuation of 249 pounds (*PA Archives*, 3rd Series, Vol. 14, 15 and 16).

Like his father and brothers John and Abraham, Daniel made his living as a blacksmith. He appears on the Salford Store ledger, either working for or doing business with his brother, John, the owner of Salford Forge (1767-1779). The "one small hammer" assessed in 1785 refers to a "tilt hammer (or plating mill) at which bar iron from the forges was hammered into sheet iron or tin-plate iron" (*Bulletin of Historical Society of Montgomery County*, Vol. 8). As he did not own this hammer in 1783, nor in 1786, it would appear his small industry did not last long. He probably sold it with his other property when he moved to Virginia in late 1785.

Daniel appears on a list of Non-Associators of Montgomery County (formed from Philadelphia County in 1784) for the years 1778-1779 (*PA Archives*, 2nd Series, Vol. 14, p.27). However, a note at the head of this list indicates that it was probably mislabeled and is actually a list of assessments. Many of those listed are known to have served in the Pennsylvania Militia, including many officers. Daniel appears on a list for Capt. Philip Reed's Company, 6th Battalion, PA Militia, for the year

1777 (*PA Archives*, 3rd Series, Vol. 15, p.762), along with most of the men living in Marlborough Township.

We know that Daniel's wife was Catherina/Catherine. Her first name appears in the baptism records of her children in Upper Salford, both at Old Goshenhoppen Reformed Church and the Lutheran Congregation of Old Goshenhoppen. Daniel and Catharina were also Sponsors or Witnesses at many of the baptisms of their friends' offspring, including neighbors Henrich (Henry) Schneider and wife Christina (1776, Lutheran), George Sheid and wife Anna Maria (1782, Reformed), and Christian Sheid and wife Maria Elisabeth (1783, Reformed). (Henry Schneider and Christian Sheid both served with Daniel in Capt. Philip Reed's Company in the Revolutionary War.)

Other researchers have given Catherine's surname as Berger, though no marriage record has been found to offer proof. Jacob Berger lived at Krider's (Salford) Forge between 1769 and 1774, according to an entry in the Salford Store Ledger, placing him there when John Krider was Forgemaster. Jacob Berger and wife Christina were witnesses to the baptism of Daniel and Catherine's son, Daniel, Jr., in the Lutheran Congregation of Old Goshenhoppen Church, April, 1770. Jacob Berger moved to Pittsylvania County, Virginia, about 1779; Daniel Krider became his neighbor a few years later (see below). Due to their ages, we may assume that Catherine was the sister of Jacob Berger, although proof has not yet been located.

There is a deed dated August 31, 1785, "from Jacob Dasht and Catherine, his wife, and Daniel Kreiter of Marlborough Township of the county of Montgomery in the Commonwealth of Pennsylvania, Yeoman, of the one part and Sebastian Goetz of the same place, Powdermaker, of the other part..." conveying 113 acres. Dasht purchased this land August 26, 1783, from Isaac Sumney and wife Magdelena. He later "sold but not actually conveyed" the parcel to Daniel Krider. This land in Marlborough Township bordered the property of Henry Schneider, Christian Sheid, Samuel Burkey and Henry Bamburger. The witnesses were Michael Croll, the owner of Salford Store, and Zebulon Potts. (Deed Book 1, page 476).

Daniel Krider moved his family to Virginia soon after he sold the land in Marlborough Township. On January 10, 1786, Daniel purchased a 500 acre parcel in Pittsylvania County from Jeremiah Ward (Deed Book 7, p.561). He also reportedly purchased an additional 260 acres from Peyton Ward (Deed Book 7, p.688). Either one or both parcels of land were situated on the north side of the Pigg River. On April 10, 1790 he purchased 500 acres on Frying Pan Creek from Anne Cornelius and others (Deed Book 8, p. 526). This was the site of "Crider's Mill," well known in the history of Pittsylvania County.

Daniel's last name evolved from Krider/Kreider/Krauter to Crider once he moved to Virginia. The family uses that spelling to this day.

According to Herman Melton, author of *18th Century Grist Mills of Pittsylvania County*, Dan Crider's mill was a landmark on the Frying Pan Creek. Dan first applied to build the mill in November of 1791 in the area of Toshes. After some calamity (probably a flood) destroyed his first mill, Dan applied to build another mill 24 years later. It was not approved until June, 1817. This mill was probably within sight of the village of Toshes and just upstream of "Boiling Springs," a ten-minute walk from the village. Siloam Methodist Church was built "on the road from Samuel Berger's Store to Daniel Crider's Mill" (state route 799) (*The History of Pittsylvania County*, Maude C. Clement). The Berger's store was directly across the street from the Berger Cemetery and next door to the home of Samuel Berger, grandson of Jacob Berger. Samuel's home has been completely restored and is occupied today by Mr. and Mrs. Thomas Jefferson. No remnants of the mill exist today, except perhaps for a rock wall on the banks of the creek which may be the ruins of the mill.

An interesting deed appeared in Pittsylvania Deed Book 9, p. 220, dated June 22, 1787, which reads: "Jacob Dasht of Marlborough Township,

Montgomery County, Pennsylvania, ironmaster, to his only son, George Dasht of the same, bachelor, for the personal affection he has for his son...a certain tract of 300 acres of land with an improvement, situated in Pittsylvania County, as the equal half part of a tract of 300 acres which is adjoining the land of Mitchel, Daniel Kreydor (sic) and Jacob Berger and others, upon condition that said tract of 600 acres shall be divided into two equal parts...George can choose which part he wants...Jacob Dasht, the father, intends in a short time also to move to Virginia, and come to live on the land. So he therefore reserves the right to build a small forge or ironwork on his son's 300 acre tract..." if it was the more desirable of the two. George agreed to support his parents if they were no longer able to support themselves "...for the rest of their lives." The deed was signed by Jacob and George Dasht, George Geiger and Michael Gutherman. It would appear that Jacob Dasht and Daniel Krider were acquainted through their common work as blacksmiths in Marlborough Township. Perhaps Jacob made the journey to Virginia with Daniel, purchased the 600 acres, then returned home to retrieve his family. (Jacob Dasht died in an accident in his blackpowder mill in Montgomery County in 1790 according to the records of Edwin Benner, published in *The Perkiomen Region,* Vol. 2, No. 3) Also, this deed places Jacob Berger and Daniel Krider as neighbors in Pittsylvania County, furthering the assumption that Daniel's wife was Jacob's relation.

Daniel Kriter, Sr. (sic), deeded land on both sides of the Buck Branch of Frying Pan Creek to Samuel Benigh, April 21, 1794 (Deed Book 9, p.549). Catherine Krider relinquished her right of dower. The deed was signed by Daniel Crider and witnessed by John Smith, Alexander Barron, and John Ward.

Dan died intestate shortly before September, 1835, in Pittsylvania County. He left an estate inventoried at a value of $4,893.45, not including his home and land. He owned 13 slaves that were valued at a total of $4,470, leaving only $423.45 for the remainder of the estate including household goods and livestock. The estate was put up for sale prior to March 9, 1836 when it was recorded (Accounts Current, Vol. 11, p. 425). Another sale was recorded Aug. 21, 1837, (ibid., p. 441). However, when his wife, Catherine, died in 1839, she left seven slaves and a considerable estate (Accounts Current, Vol. 13, p. 195).

It is presumed Catharina, or Catherine, was the sister of Jacob Berger as they were near the same age and both had lived in Philadelphia County, Pennsylvania, before moving to Pittsylvania County, Virginia.

According to family history as recorded in Pittsylvania County, Jacob and Catherine's father, "Jonathan" (probably Johannes or Hans), was born in Switzerland but his children were born in Germany. Jonathan took the family to America in 1755, arriving at the Port of Philadelphia (no emigration record has been found). Catharina would have been about six years old at emigration. Her place of birth was given by another researcher, but proof has not yet been established.

♥   Daniel married CATHARINA BERGER Bef. 1766 in Philadelphia Co., Pennsylvania.

Children of DANIEL KRIDER and CATHARINA BERGER are:

   i.   JACOB3 CRIDER, b. 1767, Philadelphia Co., Pennsylvania; d. 1843, Crittenden Co., Kentucky.

  ii. DANIEL CRIDER , JR., b. February 14, 1770, Philadelphia Co., Pennsylvania; d. May 16, 1857, Crittenden Co., Kentucky.

 iii. JOHANNES CRIDER, b. November 1771, Philadelphia Co., Pennsylvania; d. Bef. March 26, 1775, Upper Salford, Philadelphia Co., Pennsylvania. Christened: November 17, 1771, Old Goshenhoppen, Upper Salford, Philadelphia Co., Pennsylvania. Buried: April 3, 1775, Old Goshenhoppen, Upper Salford, Philadelphia Co., Pennsylvania

Johannes, son of Daniel Kreiter, was baptized at Old Goshenhoppen Reformed Church in Upper Salford Township,

Montgomery County. The sponsors were Henrich Sander and wife (*Pennsylvania German Church Records*, Vol. 3, p. 393).

According to the Church Record of Old Goshenhoppen Lutheran, Johannes, Daniel Kreuther's son, was buried in the "local cemetery", April 3, 1775. When he died he was aged 3 years, 4 months, and 9 days. Counting backwards from his burial, that would give a birthdate of November 25, 1771, which is after his known christening date. Mathematically we must therefore assume that he died prior to March 26, 1771. (LDS Microfilm)

    iv. ANDREW CRIDER, b. November 25, 1773, Philadelphia Co., Pennsylvania; d. 1856, Tennessee.

    v. JOHN CRIDER, b. 1777, Philadelphia Co., Pennsylvania; d. 1834, Pittsylvania Co., Virginia.

    vi. GEORGE CRIDER, b. 1779, Philadelphia Co., Pennsylvania; d. December 1837, Bradford, Gibson Co., Tennessee.

10.   vii. HENRY CRIDER, b. March 20, 1781, Philadelphia Co., Pennsylvania; d. 1853, Carroll Co., Tennessee.

11.   viii. SAMUEL CRIDER, b. April 21, 1783, Philadelphia Co., Pennsylvania; d. April 24, 1843, Crittenden Co., Kentucky.

12.   ix. CATHERINE CRIDER, b. September 22, 1784, Montgomery Co., Pennsylvania; d. Abt. 1852, Carroll Co., Tennessee.

13.   x. DAVID CRIDER, b. Abt. 1789, Pittsylvania Co., Virginia; d. Aft. 1860, Illinois.

14.   xi. WILLIAM B. CRIDER, b. Abt. 1791, Pittsylvania Co., Virginia; d. Aft. June 19, 1871, Pittsylvania Co., Virginia.

THIRD GENERATION

5. JACOB3 CRIDER *(DANIEL2 KRIDER, JOHN MICHAEL1 KREIDER)* was born in 1767 in Philadelphia Co., Pennsylvania, and died in 1843 in Crittenden Co., Kentucky.

Jacob received a 400 acre land grant on the Piney Fork-Tradewater watercourse in Livingston County on January 15, 1807. This section of Livingston County became Crittenden County in 1842.

♥ Jacob married MARY REITTER January 14, 1790 in Pittsylvania Co., Virginia, daughter of JOHANNE REITTER.

Children of JACOB CRIDER and MARY REITTER are:

	i.	JOHN4 CRIDER, b. 1791, Pittsylvania Co., Virginia; d. in Kentucky; m. REBECCA HOLMAN, January 7, 1812, Livingston Co., Kentucky.
15.	ii.	MARY POLLY CRIDER, b. April 14, 1792, Pittsylvania Co., Virginia; d. 1854, Crittenden Co., Kentucky.
16.	iii.	CATHERINE CRIDER, b. March 19, 1794, Pittsylvania Co., Virginia; d. August 15, 1859, Crittenden Co., Kentucky.
17.	iv.	ELIZABETH "BETSY" CRIDER, b. October 12, 1796, Pittsylvania Co., Virginia; d. October 10, 1834, Livingston Co., Kentucky.
18.	v.	JACOB B. CRIDER, b. September 30, 1798, Pittsylvania Co., Virginia; d. August 4, 1875, Caldwell Co., Kentucky.
19.	vi.	SAMUEL J. CRIDER, b. December 27, 1804, Pittsylvania Co., Virginia; d. March 6, 1879, Crittenden Co., Kentucky.
	vii.	SARAH CRIDER, b. 1810, Pittsylvania Co., Virginia; d. February 1823, Caldwell Co., Kentucky; m. JOHN MILLER, in Kentucky.

20.   viii.   WILLIAM M. CRIDER, b. October 29, 1811, Livingston Co.,
                Kentucky; d. July 30, 1886, Crittenden Co., Kentucky.

6. DANIEL3 CRIDER , JR. *(DANIEL2 KRIDER, JOHN MICHAEL1 KREIDER)* was born February 14, 1770 in Philadelphia Co., Pennsylvania, and died May 16, 1857 in Crittenden Co., Kentucky. Christened: April 30, 1770, Old Goshenhoppen, Philadelphia Co., Pennsylvania.

When Daniel, son of Daniel Kreyter and wife Catharina, was baptized in the Lutheran Congregation of Old Goshenhoppen Church in Upper Salford, the sponsors Jacob Berger and his wife, Christina (*The Perkiomen Region*, Vol. 2, No. 3, p. 56).

Daniel Crider took his family to Greenville Co., South Carolina, before 1800 as they appear on the census of that year. About 1806 they relocated to Caldwell Co., Kentucky.

♥ Daniel married NANCY BENNETT March 31, 1790 in Pittsylvania Co., Virginia, daughter of THOMAS BENNETT and MARGARET ROYSDON.

   Children of DANIEL CRIDER and NANCY BENNETT are:

      i.   MARY POLLY4 CRIDER, b. 1791, Pittsylvania Co., Virginia;
            m. JOLLY JONES, July 28, 1809, Livingston Co., Kentucky.
      ii.   WILLIAM WASHINGTON CRIDER, b. 1792, Pittsylvania Co.,
            Virginia; d. Alabama; m. POLLY KILLOUGH, October 4, 1813,
            Livingston Co., Kentucky.
      iii. JOHN CRIDER, b. Abt. 1793, Pittsylvania Co., Virginia; m.
            ELIZABETH SON, February 25, 1811, Livingston Co.,
            Kentucky.

21. iv. HENRY CRIDER, b. February 21, 1795, Pittsylvania Co.,
            Virginia; d. July 12, 1840, Livingston Co., Kentucky.
      v. CATHERINE CRIDER, b. Abt. 1796, Pittsylvania Co., Virginia;
            d. Aft. 1860, Hardin Co., Illinois; m. ROBERT HALEZ, June 27,
            1813, Livingston Co., Kentucky.
      vi. RACHEL CRIDER, b. 1798, Pittsylvania Co., Virginia; m.
            ISAAC SIMPSON, May 19, 1818, Livingston Co., Kentucky.
22. vii. DAVID CRIDER, b. Abt. 1800, Pittsylvania Co., Virginia; d.
            Abt. 1849, Crittenden Co., Kentucky.
23. viii. THOMAS BENNETT CRIDER, b. 1806, Livingston Co.,
            Kentucky.
      ix. NANCY CRIDER, b. 1810, Livingston Co., Kentucky; m. JOHN
            TRAVIS, September 22, 1829, Livingston Co., Kentucky.
      x. DANIEL CRIDER, b. August 1810, Livingston Co., Kentucky;
            d. June 04, 1850, Crittenden Co., Kentucky. Buried: Piney
            Fork Cem., Crittenden Co., Kentucky
24. xi. STEPHEN CRIDER, b. 1812, Livingston Co., Kentucky; d. June
            18, 1858, Crittenden Co., Kentucky.

7. ANDREW3 CRIDER *(DANIEL2 KRIDER, JOHN MICHAEL1 KREIDER)*
was born November 25, 1773 in Philadelphia Co., Pennsylvania, and
died in 1856 in Tennessee. Christened: January 24, 1774, Old
Goshenhoppen, Upper Salford, Philadelphia Co., Pennsylvania

Andrew was baptized "Andreas" in the Lutheran Congregation of Old
Goshenhoppen Church at Upper Salford Township in what is now
Montgomery County. The parents were listed as Daniel Kreuther and
wife Catherina; the Sponsors were Andreas Ohl and wife Eva (*The
Perkiomen Region*, Vol. 2, No. 3, p. 59). Andreas Ohl was an innkeeper
and prominent man in the church.

♥ Andrew married CHRISTINA DEBOE January 1, 1796, in Pittsylvania
Co., Virginia.

Children of ANDREW CRIDER and CHRISTINA DEBOE are:

   i.   ELIZABETH4 CRIDER, b. Abt. 1798, Pittsylvania Co., Virginia; m. WYATT WALLIS, December 29, 1823, Pittsylvania Co., Virginia.

   ii. SARAH CRIDER, b. Abt. 1800, Pittsylvania Co., Virginia; m. HENRY TOLER, January 29, 1833, Pittsylvania Co., Virginia.

         Henry was the son of Elijah and Polly Toler according to his marriage bond.

   iii. NANCY CRIDER, b. Abt. 1802, Pittsylvania Co., Virginia; m. WILLIAM TOSH, October 1823, Pittsylvania Co., Virginia.

   iv. CATHERINE CRIDER, b. Abt. 1805, Pittsylvania Co., Virginia; m. LEWIS BOBBITT, January 20, 1840, Pittsylvania Co., Virginia.

         When Catherine married Lewis Bobbitt, the bondsman was her father, Andrew Crider. The marriage was performed by Joel T. Adams.

8. JOHN3 CRIDER *(DANIEL2 KRIDER, JOHN MICHAEL1 KREIDER)* was born in 1777 in Philadelphia Co., Pennsylvania, and died in 1834 in Pittsylvania Co., Virginia. Christened: April 24, 1777, Old Goshenhoppen, Upper Salford, Philadelphia Co., Pennsylvania

John, son of Daniel Krauter, was baptized "Johannes" in Old Goshenhoppen Reformed Church. The sponsors were his uncle John Krider (Joh. Krauter) and wife (*Pennsylvania German Church Records*, Vol. 3). Apparently, John was the second child by that name but the only one to survive childhood.

♥ John married CATHERINE CRAFT January 13, 1803, in Pittsylvania Co., Virginia.

Catherine's father, according to the marriage bond, was Jacob Groft. This surname is given as Groff, Groft, Croft, and Craft. It has not been researched sufficiently to determine which is the correct spelling.

Children of JOHN CRIDER and CATHERINE CRAFT are:

25.   i.   HENRY4 CRIDER, b. Abt. 1801, Pittsylvania Co., Virginia; d. August 19, 1834, Pittsylvania Co., Virginia.

        ii. DANIEL CRIDER, b. July 18, 1807, Pittsylvania Co., Virginia; d. November 02, 1859, Pittsylvania Co., Virginia; m. CATHERINE J. ROHRER, October 07, 1837, Pittsylvania Co., Virginia. Buried: Cheva Church, Pittsylvania Co., Virginia

Daniel made his living as a blacksmith, according to *Some Death Dates of the Period 1853-1896, Pittsylvania County, Virginia.*

Daniel Crider wrote his will in Pittsylvania County, Jan. 24, 1856. He mentioned mother Catherine, wife Catherine J., brother Henry and his son Henry, brothers William, Jacob, and David. The witnesses were David Graves, Samuel Berger, W. R. Berger, Daniel G. Berger and John M. Pullen. Apparently, Daniel had no children.

26.   iii. JACOB R. CRIDER, b. Abt. 1809, Pittsylvania Co., Virginia; d. Abt. 1874, Caldwell Co., Kentucky.

        iv. WILLIAM CRIDER , JR., b. 1811, Pittsylvania Co., Virginia; d. Aft. 1860, Pittsylvania Co., Virginia; m. HARRIETT E. EDWARDS, October 7, 1863, Pittsylvania Co., Virginia.

In the 1860 census of Pittsylvania County, William, age 48, was living in the home of his brother, David, and his family. William's occupation was given as "blacksmith," sticking with the Crider tradition.

William married for the first time at age 52 to Harriet Edwards. He was listed as the son of John and Catherine Crider in the marriage register.

William's wife, Harriet, was living as a childless widow in the home of her brother-in-law, David Crider, in the 1870-1880 census.

Harriet married for the first time at age 45. She was listed as the daughter of George A. and J. Edwards.

27.   v.   DAVID CRIDER, b. Abt. 1819, Pittsylvania Co., Virginia; d. in 1882, Pittsylvania Co., Virginia.

9. GEORGE3 CRIDER *(DANIEL2 KRIDER, JOHN MICHAEL1 KREIDER)* was born 1779 in Philadelphia Co., Pennsylvania, and died December 1837 in Bradford, Gibson Co., Tennessee. Christened: April 16, 1779, Old Goshenhoppen, Upper Salford, Philadelphia Co., Pennsylvania. Buried: Bradford, Gibson Co., Tennessee

George was baptized "Georgus, son of Daniel Krauter", at Old Goshenhoppen Reformed Church in Upper Salford Township in what is now Montgomery County. The Witnesses were Georg Dorscht (George Dasht?) and Maria Langbein *(Pennsylvania German Church Records*, Vol. 3).

George is listed in the 1820 census in Franklin County, Virginia, next to Pittsylvania County. This George appears to be too young (16-26) to be our George; however, George is not found in the census of any other Virginia, North Carolina or Tennessee county. This may be in error. In 1830 he appears in Henry County, Tennessee, northeast of Gibson County.

George was in Henry County by June 9, 1824 for on that date he was paid for "...producing seven wolf scalps in open court, and proved to the satisfaction of the Court five Justices present that he killed them within the bound of Henry County and that they were under four months old" (Henry Co. Court Min., Book A, 1824-1825, p.49). Several other men were also paid for producing wolf scalps. They were obviously a serious problem in the county. George took an active role in county affairs, serving on many a jury during this two year span.

Samuel Hawkins deeded 250 acres of land in Henry County to George Crider in the summer of 1825 (ibid, p.357). This same Samuel Hawkins was residing in Maury County, Tennessee, and leased land in Carroll County to Henry Crider in 1822 (see notes for Richard Henry Crider, son of Henry).

George died in late December, 1837. On January 1, 1838, his sons Thomas Bennett and Samuel J. were named the executors of his will. Peter Trosper and Wilson Cooper were Securities. (Gibson County Bonds and Wills, p. 210)

In February, 1838, the estate of George Crider was sued by Moses Woodfin who won a judgement for $137 plus costs. There was determined to be no personal property left behind save a tract of land purchased from W.W. Hickman. That land was situated in Gibson County "...on the waters of Rutherfords Fork of Obion River (p.324)." Moses Woodfin, as the only creditor, put a lien on this property in order to satisfy the judgement. Thomas B. Crider, "as Admr. of George Crider dec'd. and as attorney for all of said defendants save the minors and as guardian ad litem for said minors...admits all the statements contained in complaintant's bill and has no reason to urge why the prayer of the same should not be granted." The land was auctioned May 11, 1843. Moses Woodfin was the highest bidder at $232.44, the amount "due Woodfin and costs". At the beginning of this suit is a list of all the heirs of George Crider: "Thomas B. Crider, Samuel J. Crider, Daniel Crider, Charles J. Lawrence who intermarried with Catherine Crider since dec'd. and her children to wit-- Elizabeth who intermarried with George Reed, George, N.B., Leander, Thomas B., Malissa C., Sarah A., and William Lawrence, the last six named heirs being minors--Asa English and Elizabeth his wife formerly Elizabeth Crider, Josiah A. Reed and Frances his wife formerly Frances Crider, Thomas Ward and Rose his wife formerly Rose Crider, citizens of Gibson County, Tennessee, George W. Crider and David Crider citizens of the State of Kentucky and Winston B. Crider, a citizen of the State of Missouri" (Winston is shown as William B. in later records).

Frances Bennett was underage at her marriage as her father, Thomas F. Bennett, gave his consent, Dec. 31, 1802. They were married Jan. 3, 1803, in Pittsylvania County. The bondsman was Henry Crider, George's brother. The witness was William Harrison and the testator was Horatio Bennett,, who may have been a brother of Frances..

The Schedule of Property of Frances Crider, dec'd widow of George Crider, was returned by T.B. and S.J. Crider, administrators, Oct. 19, 1839 (Gibson County Records, p. 292-293). She apparently died shortly after her husband.

♥ George married FRANCES BENNETT January 3, 1803, in Pittsylvania Co., Virginia, daughter of THOMAS F. BENNETT and ELIZABETH BENNETT, born about 1785 in Pittsylvania Co., Virginia, and died in 1839 in Bradford, Gibson Co., Tennessee.

Children of GEORGE CRIDER and FRANCES BENNETT are:

28. i. DAVID4 CRIDER, b. 1804, Pittsylvania Co., Virginia; d. Abt. 1875, Graves Co., Missouri.

29. ii. CATHERINE CRIDER, b. Abt. 1805, Pittsylvania Co., Virginia; d. Bef. 1838, Gibson Co., Tennessee.

30. iii. THOMAS BENNETT CRIDER, b. April 8, 1807, Pittsylvania Co., Virginia; d. November 25, 1863, Bradford, Gibson Co., Tennessee.

iv. WILLIAM B. CRIDER, b. Abt. 1809, Pittsylvania Co., Virginia; d. Aft. 1838, Missouri.

William B. Crider is listed in a suit against his father's estate as "a citizen of the State of Missouri."

v. ELIZABETH CRIDER, b. Abt. 1811, Virginia; m. ASA ENGLISH, Bef. 1840, Tennessee.

Elizabeth is mentioned in a suit against her father's estate as the wife of Asa English.

vi. FRANCES M. CRIDER, b. Abt.. 1812, Virginia; d. Aft. 1838; m. JOSIAH ALLEN REED, August 8, 1839, Gibson Co., Tennessee.

Josiah Allen Reed is mentioned in a suit against his father-in-law's estate as the husband of Frances Crider.

31. vii. SAMUEL J. CRIDER, b. Abt. 1814, Pittsylvania Co., Virginia; d. Aft. 1860, Weakley Co., Tennessee.

32. viii. DANIEL BENNETT CRIDER, b. 1815, Virginia; d. Aft. August 8, 1870, Bradford, Gibson Co., Tennessee.

33. ix. GEORGE W. CRIDER, b. Abt. 1817, Gibson Co., Tennessee; d. Calloway Co., Kentucky.

x. ROSANNA CRIDER, b. March 23, 1819, Virginia; d. July 1, 1874, Bradford, Gibson Co., Tennessee. Buried: July 1874, Antioch Cemetery, Gibson Co., Tennessee; m. THOMAS H. WARD, September 9, 1834, Gibson Co., Tennessee.

Rosanna was also called Rosey Ann, Rosonna, and Rosie Anna.

Thomas Word/Ward was married after the death of Rosanna to S.J. (inscribed on his tombstone). He was, however, buried next to Rosanna and S.J. is not buried in Antioch Cemetery. Buried: April 1892, Antioch Cemetery, Gibson Co., Tennessee

T.H. Word was the bondsman for the marriage of Nancy Word to Thomas B. Crider.

10. HENRY3 CRIDER *(DANIEL2 KRIDER, JOHN MICHAEL1 KREIDER)* was born March 20, 1781 in Philadelphia Co., Pennsylvania. Christened: May 20, 1781, Old Goshenhoppen, Upper Salford, Philadelphia Co., Pennsylvania and died 1853 in Carroll Co., Tennessee.

Henry was baptized "Henrich" in the Lutheran Congregation of Old Goshenhoppen Church, Upper Salford Township, in what is now Montgomery County. His parents were listed as Daniel Kreuther and wife Catherina; the Sponsors were Henrich Schneider and wife Christina *(The Perkiomen Region*, Vol. 2, No. 4, p. 78). Henrich Schneider was a shoemaker in Marlborough Township.

Henry Crider and wife Permelia lived in Smith County, 1816 to 1822, then moved on to Carroll County, Tennessee. Their first homestead was on Sandy River where the location on Beaver Creek, about a mile northeast of Hampton Cemetery *(The Holladay Family*, Alvis Milton Holladay, 1983).

When Henry died, he left a large estate including four slaves named Wyatt, Jack, Perliney and Mary. Wyatt had formerly worked for Capt. John Lee, who left him to Henry and Emaline in his will. Emaline's sister, Matilda Holland, testified that John Lee died about two years after Henry moved to Tennessee, and her father loaned property (including slaves) to Crider rather than giving them to him because he heard that Henry "...sometimes gambled and that he fixed it so that he might have the benefit of it during their lifetimes and then to be equally divided amongst my sister's children." Elijah W. Cornwell, Justice of the Peace for Smith County, certified the deposition.

An excellent source for the life and descendants of Henry Crider is a book by Alvis Milton Holladay, The Holladay Family, privately published in 1983. He gives excellent data and sources for researchers of these connected families.

♥ Henry married PERMELIA LEE October 17, 1805, in Pittsylvania Co., Virginia, daughter of JOHN LEE and TABITHA EARLY, born in 1786 in Campbell Co., Virginia, and died Nov. 27, 1849, in Carroll Co., Tennessee.

Children of HENRY CRIDER and PERMELIA LEE are:

	i.	ELIZABETH ANN4 CRIDER, b. November 12, 1806, Pittsylvania Co., Virginia; d. May 10, 1853, Henderson Co., Tennessee. Buried: Wilson Cemetery, Henderson Co., Tennessee; m. DAVID WILSON, August 19, 1841, Tennessee.
	ii.	MATILDA SUSANNE CRIDER, b. June 24, 1808, Pittsylvania Co., Virginia; d. Aft. 1860, Weakley Co., Tennessee; m. ROBERT HILLIARD, 1827, Carroll Co., Tennessee.
	iii.	SOPHIA AGNES CRIDER, b. August 26, 1810, Pittsylvania Co., Virginia; d. Madison Co., Tennessee; m. FELIX RUTHERFORD, 1831, Carroll Co., Tennessee.
34.	iv.	WILLIAM AIRE CRIDER, b. November 10, 1812, Pittsylvania Co., Virginia; d. October 5, 1884, Carroll Co., Tennessee.
	v.	NARCISSUS CRIDER, b. 1814, Pittsylvania Co., Virginia; d. Abt. 1814, Pittsylvania Co., Virginia.
	vi.	BELBEDERRA CRIDER, b. February 4, 1815, Pittsylvania Co., Virginia; d. March 15, 1817, Smith Co., Tennessee.
35.	vii.	RICHARD HENRY CRIDER, b. August 07, 1817, Smith Co., Tennessee; d. November 12, 1903, Carroll Co., Tennessee.
36.	viii.	CATHERINE CRIDER, b. May 4, 1819, Smith Co., Tennessee; d. October 14, 1914, Carroll Co., Tennessee.
37.	ix.	EMALINE CRIDER, b. March 20, 1821, Smith Co., Tennessee; d. November 12, 1898, Carroll Co., Tennessee.
38.	x.	JAMES CARROLL CRIDER, b. March 11, 1824, Carroll Co., Tennessee; d. Abt. 1895, Carroll Co., Tennessee.

39.   xi.   JOHN DANIEL CRIDER, b. February 15, 1826, Carroll Co.,
              Tennessee; d. August 31, 1904, Carroll Co., Tennessee.
40.   xii.   ANDREW JACKSON CRIDER, b. September 24, 1829, Carroll
              Co., Tennessee; d. June 1, 1906, Hempstead Co., Arkansas.

11. SAMUEL3 CRIDER *(DANIEL2 KRIDER, JOHN MICHAEL1 KREIDER)*
was born April 21, 1783 in Philadelphia Co., Pennsylvania, and died
April 24, 1843 in Crittenden Co., Kentucky.

Samuel's birth record has been given by another researcher. His baptism
has not been found by this researcher.

♥ Samuel married MARY POLLY DEBOE June 15, 1807, in Pittsylvania
Co., Virginia, born in 1786 in Pennsylvania and died in Nov, 1869, in
Caldwell Co., Tennessee.

Children of SAMUEL CRIDER and MARY DEBOE are:

       i.   ELIZABETH "BETSY"4 CRIDER, b. Abt. 1808, Pittsylvania Co.,
              Virginia.
41.   ii.   DANIEL W. CRIDER, b. February 27, 1809, Pittsylvania Co.,
              Virginia; d. April 25, 1839, Livingston Co., Kentucky.
42.   iii. FINIS EWING CRIDER, b. December 1, 1818, Livingston Co.,
              Kentucky; d. January 21, 1881, Jefferson Co., Illinois.
43.   iv.   WILLIAM H. CRIDER, b. Abt. 1819, Livingston Co., Kentucky.
       v.   MARY CRIDER, b. 1822, Livingston Co., Kentucky; m. JOSEPH
              McDOWELL, February 12, 1840, Livingston Co., Kentucky.
       vi.   PERMELIA CRIDER, b. May 21, 1823, Livingston Co.,
              Kentucky; m. JOHN McDOWELL, October 21, 1840,
              Livingston Co., Kentucky.
44.   vii. SAMUEL F. CRIDER, b. Abt. 1828, Livingston Co., Kentucky;
              d. September 10, 1856, Crittenden Co., Kentucky.

12. CATHERINE3 CRIDER *(DANIEL2 KRIDER, JOHN MICHAEL1 KREIDER)* was born September 22, 1784 in Montgomery Co., Pennsylvania. Christened: October 10, 1784, Old Goshenhoppen, Upper Salford, Montgomery Co., Pennsylvania. Died Abt.. 1852 in Carroll Co., Tennessee.

Catherine was baptized "Catharina" in the Lutheran Congregation of Old Goshenhoppen Church, Upper Salford Township, in what is now Montgomery County. Her parents were listed as Daniel Kreuther and wife Catharina; the Sponsors were Jacob Dascht and wife Catharina (*The Perkiomen Region*, Vol. 2, No. 4, p. 80). Jacob Dascht is mentioned in the notes for Daniel Krider.

♥ Catherine married MARTIN DALTON June 20, 1803, in Pittsylvania Co., Virginia, son of MARTIN DALTON and CATHERINE. He died in 1840 in Carroll Co., Tennessee.

Martin Dalton "started to Tennessee Oct. 6, 1813," according to the Dalton Register, a ledger kept by Winston Dalton, school master, in Pittsylvania County, Virginia.

Children of CATHERINE CRIDER and MARTIN DALTON are:

    i.   JOHN4 DALTON, b. January 22, 1804, Pittsylvania Co., Virginia; m. COLEY MATTOX, December 12, 1826, Pittsylvania Co., Virginia.

           John's birthdate was found in the Dalton Register, a record of important dates recorded by school master Winston Dalton in Pittsylvania County.

    ii. DANIEL DALTON, b. February 23, 1805, Pittsylvania Co., Virginia.

Daniel's birthdate was also found in the Dalton Register (see notes for his brother).

13. DAVID3 CRIDER *(DANIEL2 KRIDER, JOHN MICHAEL1 KREIDER)* was born Abt. 1789 in Pittsylvania Co., Virginia, and died Aft. 1860 in Illinois.

♥ David married POLLY VANCE February 10, 1810, in Pittsylvania Co., Virginia.

Children of DAVID CRIDER and POLLY VANCE are:

  i. GILLA4 CRIDER, b. 1812, Kentucky; d. Aft. 1860, Randolph Co., Illinois; m. JAMES BARBER, 1833, Illinois.
  ii. CATHERINE CRIDER, b. Abt. 1814, Kentucky; d. Aft. 1860, Randolph Co., Illinois; m. JAMES BARROW, 1834, Illinois.

14. WILLIAM B.3 CRIDER *(DANIEL2 KRIDER, JOHN MICHAEL1 KREIDER)* was born Abt.. 1791 in Pittsylvania Co., Virginia, and died Aft. June 19, 1871 in Pittsylvania Co., Virginia.

William Crider wrote his will June 23, 1864, in Pittsylvania County. He mentioned his son Peyton W., daughters Permelia Frances Hatchett, Cecelia A. Shelhorse, Susan C. Shelhorse, and his deceased daughter Melissa Elizabeth Gregory, her husband William Gregory and their two daughters, Carline (Caroline?) and Angoline (Angeline?) Gregory, who were both under 20 years of age. The executors were Peyton Crider and William Shelhorse. The witnesses were George T. Berger and J.D. Hank. The will was proved June 19, 1871.

♥ William married CELIA YOUNG January 6, 1814, in Pittsylvania Co., Virginia, daughter of PEYTON YOUNG.

Children of WILLIAM CRIDER and CELIA YOUNG are:

    i. PEYTON W.4 CRIDER, b. 1815, Pittsylvania Co., Virginia; d. Bef. April 15, 1878, Pittsylvania Co., Virginia.

          Peyton's will was proven will April 15, 1878, (Will Book 3, p. 214).

    ii. PERMELIA FRANCES CRIDER, b. Abt. 1820, Pittsylvania Co., Virginia; m. EDWARD HATCHETT, December 2, 1846, Pittsylvania Co., Virginia.

45.   iii. MELISSA ELIZABETH CRIDER, b. February 28, 1826, Pittsylvania Co., Virginia; d. Bef. June 1864, Pittsylvania Co., Virginia.

    iv. CECELIA ADELINE CRIDER, b. October 7, 1831, Pittsylvania Co., Virginia; m. WILLIAM H. SHELHORSE, September 10, 1857, Pittsylvania Co., Virginia.

          William H. Shelhorse was listed as the son of Jacob and Mary Shelhorse in his marriage register.

46.   v. SUSAN C. CRIDER, b. 1836, Pittsylvania Co., Virginia.

FOURTH GENERATION

15. MARY POLLY4 CRIDER *(JACOB3, DANIEL2 KRIDER, JOHN MICHAEL1 KREIDER)* was born April 14, 1792 in Pittsylvania Co., Virginia, and died 1854 in Crittenden Co., Kentucky.

♥ Polly married GEORGE GREEN December 7, 1818, in Livingston Co., Kentucky. He was born Jan. 8, 1792, and died in 1886 in Crittenden Co., Kentucky.

Children of MARY CRIDER and GEORGE GREEN are:

	i.	PEGGY5 GREEN, b. 1815, Pittsylvania Co., Virginia. Married ARMISTEAD BUTLER, Kentucky.
47.	ii.	JACOB GREEN, b. November 13, 1817, Pittsylvania Co., Virginia; d. September 1, 1837, Crittenden Co., Kentucky.
	iii.	DAVID MCLINN GREEN, b. 1820, Pittsylvania Co., Virginia. Married ELIZA LOVE, Kentucky.
	iv.	MATILDA GREEN, b. May 2, 1822, Livingston Co., Kentucky; d. June 2, 1872, Crittenden Co., Kentucky. Buried: Piney Fork Cem., Crittenden Co., Kentucky. Married DAVID ALLEN BUTLER, Livingston Co., Kentucky. David was also buried at Piney Fork Cem., Crittenden Co., Kentucky
	v.	POLLY ANN GREEN, b. April 30, 1831, Livingston Co., Kentucky; d. February 15, 1849, Crittenden Co., Kentucky. Buried: Piney Fork Cem., Crittenden Co., Kentucky. Married. WILLIAM H. CRAWFORD, Kentucky.
	vi.	LOUISA JANE GREEN, b. Abt. 1833, Livingston Co., Kentucky. Married EDWARD GROOMS, Kentucky.
	vii.	GEORGE BERRY GREEN, b. Abt. 1835, Livingston Co., Kentucky. Married ELIZA BUGG, Kentucky.

16. CATHERINE4 CRIDER *(JACOB3, DANIEL2 KRIDER, JOHN MICHAEL1 KREIDER)* was born March 19, 1794, in Pittsylvania Co., Virginia, and died August 15, 1859, in Crittenden Co., Kentucky. Buried: Piney Fork Cem., Crittenden Co., Kentucky

♥ Catherine married her cousin, HENRY CRIDER, December 13, 1813, in Livingston Co., Kentucky, son of DANIEL CRIDER and NANCY BENNETT. He was born Feb. 21, 1795, in Pittsylvania Co., Virginia, and died July 12, 1840, at Livingston Co., Kentucky. Buried at Piney Fork Cemetery, Crittenden Co., Kentucky.

Children of CATHERINE CRIDER and HENRY CRIDER are:

	i.	MARY POLLY5 CRIDER, b. April 13, 1817, Livingston Co., Kentucky; d. January 21, 1894, Belle Rive, Illinois; m. JOHN ROBERT HUGHEY, April 23, 1835, Livingston Co., Kentucky. Buried: Flint Cemetery, Belle Rive, Illinois
48.	ii.	JOHN HENRY CRIDER, b. November 12, 1819, Livingston Co., Kentucky; d. September 29, 1851, Crittenden Co., Kentucky.
49.	iii.	ELIZABETH CRIDER, b. 1821, Livingston Co., Kentucky; d. Abt. 1847, Crittenden Co., Kentucky
50.	iv.	NANCY CRIDER, b. Abt. 1825, Livingston Co., Kentucky; d. Bef. 1860.
51.	v.	WILLIAM BENNETT CRIDER, b. April 10, 1828, Livingston Co., Kentucky; d. October 26, 1910, Crittenden Co., Kentucky.
52.	vi.	RACHEL T. CRIDER, b. November 19, 1831, Livingston Co., Kentucky; d. March 27,1859, at Crittenden Co., Kentucky. Buried at Piney Fork Cemetery, Crittenden Co., Kentucky.
	vii.	SARAH A. CATHERINE CRIDER, b. September 28, 1833, Livingston Co., Kentucky; d. April 1, 1918, Crittenden Co., Kentucky; m. JOHN C. JAMES, February 10, 1852, Crittenden Co., Kentucky. b. Oct. 3, 1830 at Crittenden Co., Kentucky; d. Oct. 18, 1904, in Kentucky. Buried: Piney Fork Cem., Crittenden Co., Kentucky 1859, Crittenden Co., Kentucky.

17. ELIZABETH "BETSY"4 CRIDER *(JACOB3, DANIEL2 KRIDER, JOHN MICHAEL1 KREIDER)* was born October 12, 1796 in Pittsylvania Co., Virginia, and died October 10, 1834 in Livingston Co., Kentucky.

♥ Betsy married WILLIAM JAMES in Livingston Co., Kentucky. He was born Oct. 14, 1801, and died on Oct. 21, 1879, in Livingston Co., Kentucky.

Children of ELIZABETH CRIDER and WILLIAM JAMES are:

	i.	BETSY5 JAMES, b. Abt. 1820, Livingston Co., Kentucky.
	ii.	REBECCA JAMES, b. Abt. 1822, Livingston Co., Kentucky.
53.	iii.	JACOB JAMES, b. December 2, 1825, Crittenden Co., Kentucky; d. April 26, 1906, Kentucky, Kentucky.
	iv.	JOHN C. JAMES, b. October 3, 1830, Crittenden Co., Kentucky; d. October 18, 1904, Kentucky, Kentucky. Buried: Piney Fork Cem., Crittenden Co., Kentucky. Married SARAH A. CATHERINE CRIDER, February 10, 1852, Crittenden Co., Kentucky.

18. JACOB B.4 CRIDER *(JACOB3, DANIEL2 KRIDER, JOHN MICHAEL1 KREIDER)* was born September 30, 1798, in Pittsylvania Co., Virginia, and died August 4, 1875, in Caldwell Co., Kentucky.

Jacob B. Crider was the first Crider to live in Caldwell County, Kentucky. He came to Kentucky with his parents when he was seven years old, settling in what is now Crittenden County. He moved to Caldwell County in 1835, settling on two hundred acres in Fredonia. He added another 500 acres at a later date. He raised stock and shipped them to New Orleans. After he divided his farm among his children, he went into business with F.H. Baker as a merchant. He also ran steam flour mill "with wool carding attachments." (Cynthia Kay Crider Whitsett, *Caldwell Co. Heritage Book*).

♥ Jacob married ORPHA BIVENS Bef. 1825 in Kentucky. Orpha was born in 1797 in Georgia and died Jan.1, 1863, in Caldwell Co., Kentucky.

Children of JACOB CRIDER and ORPHA BIVENS are:

     i. ZACHARIAH JOHNSON5 CRIDER, b. December 23, 1825, Caldwell Co., Kentucky; d. 1911, Crider, Caldwell Co., Kentucky. Buried: 1911, Bethlehem Cem., Crider, Caldwell Co., Kentucky. m. ELIZABETH JANE KIRKPATRICK, February 9, 1858, Caldwell Co., Kentucky. She was buried in 1915, Bethlehem Cem., Crider, Caldwell Co., Kentucky

        Zachariah lived on the family farm until the age of twenty when he became a merchant in Fredonia. In 1868 he moved to a settlement known as "Walnut Grove" where the town of Crider is now located (named after him). He owned 700 acres there and raised crops on 600 of them, raising stock on the side. In 1876 he purchased Hoover Mill, a flour mill, and operated a store for a few years. Zachariah and wife Jane had no children of their own but reared the children of his sister, Louisa Myers (Cynthia Kay Crider Whitsett, *Caldwell County Heritage Book*).

     ii. MARY JANE CRIDER, b. Abt. 1827, Kentucky; m. JOHN WYATT, Kentucky.
     iii. ELIZA CRIDER, b. Abt. 1829, Kentucky; m. JOHN MYERS, Kentucky.
54.   iv. JACOB EWING CRIDER, b. May 25, 1842, Princeton, Caldwell Co., Kentucky; d. 1927, Caldwell Co., Kentucky.

19. SAMUEL J.4 CRIDER *(JACOB3, DANIEL2 KRIDER, JOHN MICHAEL1 KREIDER)* was born December 27, 1804, in Pittsylvania Co., Virginia, and died March 6, 1879, in Crittenden Co., Kentucky.

S.J. Crider had a lamb with five legs and six feet, according to the Marion Reporter (newspaper), June 8, 1881.

♥ Samuel married (1) POLLY R. FOSTER October 3, 1827, in Livingston Co., Kentucky, daughter of SAMUEL FOSTER and SAVILITY TRAVIS. Polly was born Oct. 5, 1808, and died May 22, 1851, in Crittenden Co., Kentucky; buried at Piney Fork Cemetery, Crittenden Co., Kentucky.

Children of SAMUEL CRIDER and POLLY FOSTER are:

        i. MATILDA5 CRIDER, b. 1828, Livingston Co., Kentucky. Married. SAMUEL SCOTT, March 23, 1847, Crittenden Co., Kentucky.

55.   ii. MARY SALINA CRIDER, b. 1830, Livingston Co., Kentucky.

      iii. MALVINA ANN CRIDER, b. June 19, 1832, Livingston Co., Kentucky; d. December 9, 1910, Repton, Kentucky. m. WILLIAM H. ASHER, March 20, 1849, Crittenden Co., Kentucky.

Malvina was married at the home of her father by W.C. Love, Minister of the Gospel. The bondsman was David McDowell. William was "of age" at his marriage.

♥ Samuel married (2) MARY ANN HUGHEY Aft. March 1851 in Kentucky. She died in 1865 in Wake Co., North Carolina.

20. WILLIAM M.4 CRIDER *(JACOB3, DANIEL2 KRIDER, JOHN MICHAEL1 KREIDER)* was born October 29, 1811, in Livingston Co., Kentucky, and died July 30, 1886, in Crittenden Co., Kentucky. Buried: Piney Fork Cem., Crittenden Co., Kentucky.

William was a farmer, living in the Piney Fork section of Crittenden County. He wrote his will February 20, 1886 in Crittenden County. He mentioned children Presley Harris, William Bradley, Samuel Foster, Adaline, Emmeline, Mary Jane, Amison Alonzo, and Davis Ewing. The executor was his grandson, George H. Crider. The witnesses were W.J. Hill and James A. Price. The will was probated August 9, 1886.

This is probably the man referred to in a newspaper clipping, dated October 19, 1881, from the *Marion Reporter*: "Boss" Crider, a respectable farmer in the Piney neighborhood, has, it is supposed, lost his mind. He has been in this condition for more than a week."

Nancy's last name is given as Crayne and/or Green. It has been said the names could be the same, depending on the brogue of the speaker, resulting in the different spellings (Fay Carol Crider, *Heritage of Crittenden County, Kentucky*, p. 89.) She was the widow of James Hill when they married.

♥ William married (1) MELISSA FOSTER February 22, 1829, in Kentucky, daughter of SAMUEL FOSTER and SAVILITY TRAVIS, sister of Polly (see Samuel J. Crider). Melissa was born about 1815 in Kentucky and died in July, 1847, at Crittenden Co., Kentucky.

Children of WILLIAM CRIDER and MELISSA FOSTER are:

56.   i.   PRESLEY HARRIS5 CRIDER, b. Abt. 1830, Livingston Co., Kentucky.

57.   ii. WILLIAM BRADLEY CRIDER, b. January 20, 1831, Livingston Co., Kentucky; d. 1883, Crittenden Co., Kentucky.

58. iii. SAMUEL FOSTER CRIDER, b. August 16, 1832, Livingston Co., Kentucky; d. November 22, 1894, Crittenden Co., Kentucky.
59. iv. SERENA ADALINE CRIDER, b. April 3, 1834, Livingston Co., Kentucky; d. July 16, 1879, Crittenden Co., Kentucky.
60. v. CYNTHIA EMMELINE CRIDER, b. February 21, 1836, Livingston Co., Kentucky; d. February 17, 1866.
     vi. JACOB MARION CRIDER, b. December 5, 1838, Livingston Co., Kentucky; d. April 28, 1862, Nashville, Davidson Co., Kentucky.

Jacob probably never married. He died while serving in the Civil War, having joined the 20th Kentucky Regiment Volunteer Company at Smithland, Kentucky, October 7, 1861. He died less than seven months later.

61. vii. MARY JANE CRIDER, b. Abt. 1840, Livingston Co., Kentucky.
     viii. LOUISA M. CRIDER, b. October 10, 1845, Crittenden Co., Kentucky; d. December 5, 1886, Crittenden Co., Kentucky.

♥ William married (2) NANCY CRAYNE May 30, 1848, in Crittenden Co., Kentucky.

Children of WILLIAM CRIDER and NANCY CRAYNE are:

62. ix. AMISON ALONZO5 CRIDER, b. December 4, 1849, Crittenden Co., Kentucky; d. September 28, 1891.
63. x. DAVIS EWING CRIDER, b. July 25, 1855, Crittenden Co., Kentucky; d. February 8, 1924, Marion, Crittenden Co., Kentucky.

21. HENRY4 CRIDER *(DANIEL3, DANIEL2 KRIDER, JOHN MICHAEL1 KREIDER)* was born February 21, 1795, in Pittsylvania Co., Virginia, and died July 12, 1840, in Livingston Co., Kentucky. Buried: Piney Fork Cem., Crittenden Co., Kentucky.

♥ Henry married CATHERINE CRIDER December 13, 1813, in Livingston Co., Kentucky, daughter of JACOB CRIDER and MARY REITTER.

Descendants of this couple have already been listed under Catherine's entry.

Children of HENRY CRIDER and CATHERINE CRIDER are:

     i.   MARY POLLY5 CRIDER, b. April 13, 1817, Livingston Co., Kentucky; d. January 21, 1894, Belle Rive, Illinois; m. JOHN ROBERT HUGHEY, April 23, 1835, Livingston Co., Kentucky.

       Robert was buried: in Flint Cemetery, Belle Rive, Illinois

48.   ii. JOHN HENRY CRIDER, b. November 12, 1819, Livingston Co., Kentucky; d. September 29, 1851, Crittenden Co., Kentucky.

49.   iii. ELIZABETH CRIDER, b. 1821, Livingston Co., Kentucky; d. Abt. 1847, Crittenden Co., Kentucky.

50.   iv. NANCY CRIDER, b. Abt. 1825, Livingston Co., Kentucky; d. Bef. 1860.

51.   v. WILLIAM BENNETT CRIDER, b. April 10, 1828, Livingston Co., Kentucky; d. October 26, 1910, Crittenden Co., Kentucky.

52.   vi. RACHEL T. CRIDER, b. November 19, 1831, Livingston Co., Kentucky; d. March 27, 1859, Crittenden Co., Kentucky.

     vii. SARAH A. CATHERINE CRIDER, b. September 28, 1833, Livingston Co., Kentucky; d. April 1, 1918, Crittenden Co., Kentucky; m. JOHN C. JAMES, February 10, 1852, Crittenden Co., Kentucky. John was buried in Piney Fork Cem., Crittenden Co., Kentucky.

22. DAVID4 CRIDER *(DANIEL3, DANIEL2 KRIDER, JOHN MICHAEL1 KREIDER)* was born Abt. 1800 in Pittsylvania Co., Virginia, and died Abt. 1849 in Crittenden Co., Kentucky.

♥ David married TRESSA B. TRAVIS October 10, 1831, in Livingston Co., Kentucky. Tressa was born Nov. 12, 1812, in Crittenden Co., Kentucky, and died in Apr., 1906, in Crittenden Co., Kentucky.

Children of DAVID CRIDER and TRESSA TRAVIS are:

    i.   NANCY ELVIRA5 CRIDER, b. 1832, Kentucky; m. ISAAC L. WHEELER, October 21, 1850, Crittenden Co., Kentucky.

    ii. NEWBERN CRIDER, b. Abt. 1834, Kentucky; d. Abt. 1834, Kentucky.

    iii. EMILY GARDNER CRIDER, b. 1842, Kentucky; d. 1877; m. WILLIAM M. CLARK, October 9, 1859, Crittenden Co., Kentucky.

    iv. EWELL CRIDER, b. Abt. 1845, Kentucky; d. Abt. 1845, Kentucky.

    v. SUSAN JOAN CRIDER, b. 1848, Kentucky; d. 1904, Kentucky; m. JAMES EDWARD CROWELL, November 22, 1865, Crittenden Co., Kentucky.

23. THOMAS BENNETT4 CRIDER *(DANIEL3, DANIEL2 KRIDER, JOHN MICHAEL1 KREIDER)* was born in 1806 in Livingston Co., Kentucky.

♥ Thomas married MARY POLLY DULANEY October 26, 1826, in Livingston Co., Kentucky, daughter of WILLIAM DULANEY and SALLY TRAVIS.

Children of THOMAS CRIDER and MARY DULANEY are:

    i.   JAMES5 CRIDER, b. 1834, Livingston Co., Kentucky.
   ii. MARY CRIDER, b. 1836, Livingston Co., Kentucky.
  iii. RACHEL CRIDER, b. 1838, Livingston Co., Kentucky.
  iv. DANIEL CRIDER, b. 1841, Livingston Co., Kentucky.
64.   v. FRANKLIN CRIDER, b. 1846, Livingston Co., Kentucky.

24. STEPHEN4 CRIDER *(DANIEL3, DANIEL2 KRIDER, JOHN MICHAEL1 KREIDER)* was born in 1812 in Livingston Co., Kentucky, and died June 18, 1858, in Crittenden Co., Kentucky.

♥ Stephen married SALLY LAVINA CAROLINE BRANTLEY Nov. 8, 1834, in Livingston Co., Kentucky.

Children of STEPHEN CRIDER and SALLY BRANTLEY are:

    i.   JOHN W.5 CRIDER, b. 1836, Livingston Co., Kentucky.
   ii. L. M. CRIDER, b. 1838, Livingston Co., Kentucky.
  iii. DANIEL B. CRIDER, b. 1841, Livingston Co., Kentucky.
  iv. STEPHEN CRIDER, b. 1843, Livingston Co., Kentucky.
    v. N. J. CRIDER, b. 1844, Livingston Co., Kentucky.
  vi. MARY LAVINA CRIDER, b. 1848, Livingston Co., Kentucky.

25. HENRY4 CRIDER *(JOHN3, DANIEL2 KRIDER, JOHN MICHAEL1 KREIDER)* was born Abt. 1801 in Pittsylvania Co., Virginia, and died August 19, 1834, in Pittsylvania Co., Virginia.

Henry Crider, age 31, died at his home, according to *The Lynchburg Virginian*, Sept. 15, 1834. He is said to have "left a wife", but no mention is made of children.

♥ Henry married MATILDA BENNETT December 16, 1833, in Bedford Co., Virginia, daughter of RICHARD BENNETT and ASENATH DALTON. Matilda was born Dec. 18, 1812, at Bedford Co., Virginia, and died Dec. 21, 1867, at Toshes, Pittsylvania Co., Virginia. She was buried at Siloam Methodist Church in Toshes.

Matilda married secondly Isiah Ramsey with whom she had six children. She was buried at: Siloam Methodist Church, Toshes, Pittsylvania Co., Virginia

Child of HENRY CRIDER and MATILDA BENNETT is:

    i.   HENRY5 CRIDER, b. Aft. August 1834, Pittsylvania Co., Virginia.

        Matilda Crider was appointed to see after the interests of infant Henry Crider, son of Henry, deceased, Feb. 16, 1836. As the son was not mentioned in the obituary of Henry, Sr., perhaps he was born after his father's death.

26. JACOB R.4 CRIDER *(JOHN3, DANIEL2 KRIDER, JOHN MICHAEL1 KREIDER)* was born Abt. 1809 in Pittsylvania Co., Virginia, and died Abt. 1874 in Caldwell Co., Kentucky. Buried: Hill Cemetery, Caldwell Co., Kentucky

.♥ Jacob married (1) NANCY ROHRER December 19, 1832, in Pittsylvania Co., Virginia. Nancy was born Dec. 14, 1814, in Pittsylvania Co., Virginia, and died in June, 1839, at Caldwell Co., Kentucky.

Children of JACOB CRIDER and NANCY ROHRER are:

    i.   BABY BOY5 CRIDER, b. September 23, 1833, Pittsylvania Co., Virginia; d. 1833, Pittsylvania Co., Virginia.

       This son died while an infant, according to the Dalton Register.

    ii. SARAH CATHERINE CRIDER, b. 1835, Pittsylvania Co., Virginia; d. Aft. 1850, Crittenden Co., Kentucky; m. THOMAS C. CAMPBELL, February 10, 1853, Crittenden Co., Kentucky.

   iii. PERMILIA JANE CRIDER, b. 1837, Pittsylvania Co., Virginia; d. Aft. 1850, Crittenden Co., Kentucky.

♥ Jacob married (2) ARMILDA STOKES April 27, 1840, in Caldwell Co., Kentucky. She was born in Dec., 1818, in South Carolina, and died Dec. 8, 1891, in Caldwell Co., Kentucky.

Children of JACOB CRIDER and ARMILDA STOKES are:

   iv. JOHN B.5 CRIDER, b. 1841, Caldwell Co., Kentucky.
    v. NANCY E. CRIDER, b. 1844, Caldwell Co., Kentucky.
   vi. WILLIAM H. CRIDER, b. 1846, Caldwell Co., Kentucky.
  vii. LYSANDER CRIDER, b. 1848, Caldwell Co., Kentucky.

27. DAVID4 CRIDER *(JOHN3, DANIEL2 KRIDER, JOHN MICHAEL1 KREIDER)* was born Abt. 1819 in Pittsylvania Co., Virginia, and died in 1882 in Pittsylvania Co., Virginia.

♥ David married MARY JANE EDWARDS January 27, 1840, in Pittsylvania Co., Virginia, daughter of GEORGE A. EDWARDS.

Children of DAVID CRIDER and MARY EDWARDS are:

65.   i.   LUCY JANE5 CRIDER, b. December 19, 1840, Pittsylvania Co.,
           Virginia; d. 1903, Toshes, Pittsylvania Co., Virginia.
      ii. CATHERINE ELIZABETH CRIDER, b. 1843, Pittsylvania Co.,
           Virginia; m. JOSIAH H. TOSH, April 28, 1867, Pittsylvania
           Co., Virginia.

           Elizabeth was 24 years of age at the time of her marriage. Her
           parents were listed as David and Mary Crider.

           Josiah was 26 years old at the time of his marriage. His parents
           were listed as George and Lucy Tosh on the marriage register.
           The marriage was performed by Josiah D. Hank.

           Josiah was buried at Siloam Methodist, Toshes, Pittsylvania
           Co., Virginia.

      iii. WILLIAM D. CRIDER, b. 1845, Pittsylvania Co., Virginia; d.
           September 1862, Pittsylvania Co., Virginia.

           William died at age 17 of fever, according to his Uncle William
           Crider. His parents were given as D. and M. Crider (*Some
           Death Dates of the Period 1853-1896, Pittsylvania County,
           Virginia*).

66.   iv. GILLIE A. CRIDER, b. March 12, 1848, Pittsylvania Co.,
           Virginia; d. October 23, 1922, Toshes, Pittsylvania Co.,
           Virginia.
      v.   CORDELIA F. CRIDER, b. August 14, 1853, Pittsylvania Co.,
           Virginia; m. JOHN W. ELLIOTT, August 15, 1877, Pittsylvania
           Co., Virginia.

           John was the son of Thomas J. and Sarah E. Elliott, according
           to his marriage register. He was 22 years old when he married
           Delia F. Crider, age 23. The marriage was performed by Isiah
           Ramsey.

      vi. JUDITH CRIDER, b. December 1856, Pittsylvania Co., Virginia.

Judith, possibly also known as Virginia, was mentally handicapped ("idiotic") according to the 1880 census.

67.   vii.   GEORGE DAVID CRIDER, b. November 5, 1859, Pittsylvania Co., Virginia; d. January 31, 1929, Pittsylvania Co., Virginia.

28. DAVID4 CRIDER *(GEORGE3, DANIEL2 KRIDER, JOHN MICHAEL1 KREIDER)* was born in 1804 in Pittsylvania Co., Virginia, and died Abt. 1875 in Graves Co., Missouri.

David Crider entered 150 acres of land attached to his own 50 acre entry July 30, 1831, in Weakley County. This land bordered the property of Mr. Ross in District #12 which was located in the southeast corner of the county on the Carroll County line.

David appears in the 1830 Tennessee census in Weakley County as head of household with one female 16-30 (his wife) and one female child under five (Sarah). In 1834 his son, James A., was born in Gibson County, Tennessee. On Feb. 28, 1835, David was Bondsman for his brother Samuel's marriage to Mary Yates, also in Gibson County. In 1838 his daughter Lee Anna was born.

By 1838 David was in Kentucky as evidenced by a suit against his father's estate. Among the list of heirs, David is listed as being a citizen "of the State of Kentucky." By the 1840 census he was living in Calloway County, Kentucky.

The 1850 census, also in Calloway County, lists David's occupation as a blacksmith while son James is listed as a farmer.

By 1860 David had moved again to Graves County, Kentucky. In the 1874 tax list he owned 160 acres in Graves County and 60 acres in nearby Calloway County. He disappears from the records after 1875.

♥ He married SARAH (possibly WALKER) in Tennessee.

No marriage record has been located, but census records list David's wife as Sarah, born 1811 in Kentucky. Two of their sons bore the middle name Walker, indicating that may have been Sarah's surname. There was a Walker family in nearby Carroll County.

Children of DAVID CRIDER and SARAH are:
68. i. JAMES A.5 CRIDER, b. 1834, Gibson Co., Tennessee; d. 1875, Calloway Co., Kentucky.
69. ii. LEE ANNA CRIDER, b. 1836, Gibson Co., Tennessee.
     iii. SARAH CRIDER, b. 1838, Missouri.
70. iv. RACHEL R. CRIDER, b. October 10, 1840, Calloway Co., Kentucky.
     v. SABRINA CRIDER, b. 1846, Calloway Co., Kentucky.
71. vi. ROBERT WALKER CRIDER, b. 1848, Calloway Co., Kentucky; d. October 1880, Pocahontas, Randolph Co., Arkansas.
     vii. JOHN WALKER CRIDER, b. 1851, Calloway Co., Kentucky; d. Graves Co., Kentucky.

> John Walker Crider's family Bible was found in the LDS Microfilm #301102, *Bible Records of Western Kentucky*. The Bible was from Graves County, Kentucky.

29. CATHERINE4 CRIDER *(GEORGE3, DANIEL2 KRIDER, JOHN MICHAEL1 KREIDER)* was born Abt. 1805 in Pittsylvania Co., Virginia, and died Bef. 1838 in Gibson Co., Tennessee.

Catherine Crider was deceased by her father's death as shown by a suit against her father's estate. She is listed as the daughter of George Crider, deceased, late wife of Charles J. Lawrence. Her children are also listed.

♥ Catherine married CHARLES J. LAWRENCE May 20, 1817, in Sumner Co., Tennessee.

Charles J. Lawrence is mentioned in a suit against his father-in-law's estate, 1838, as the husband of Catherine Crider, dec'd.

Children of CATHERINE CRIDER and CHARLES LAWRENCE are:

     i.   ELIZABETH5 LAWRENCE, b. Abt. 1822, Gibson Co., Tennessee.

         Elizabeth was married and no longer a minor by 1840.

     ii.   GEORGE LAWRENCE, b. Abt. 1824, Gibson Co., Tennessee.
     iii.   N. B. LAWRENCE, b. Abt. 1826, Gibson Co., Tennessee.
     iv.   LEANDER LAWRENCE, b. Abt. 1828, Gibson Co., Tennessee.
     v.   THOMAS B. LAWRENCE, b. Abt. 1830, Gibson Co., Tennessee.
     vi.   MALISSA C. LAWRENCE, b. Abt. 1832, Gibson Co., Tennessee.
     vii.   SARAH A. LAWRENCE, b. Abt. 1834, Gibson Co., Tennessee.

         Sarah is a 16 year old in the 1850 Gibson County census, living in the home of Thomas Bennett Crider, her uncle.

     viii.   WILLIAM LAWRENCE, b. Abt. 1838, Gibson Co., Tennessee.

         In the 1850 census of Gibson County, William Lawrence is living in the home of his uncle, Thomas Bennett Crider. He is listed as being 12 years old.

30. THOMAS BENNETT4 CRIDER *(GEORGE3, DANIEL2 KRIDER, JOHN MICHAEL1 KREIDER)* was born April 8, 1807, in Pittsylvania Co., Virginia, and died November 25, 1863, in Bradford, Gibson Co.,

Tennessee. Buried: November 1863, Antioch Cem., Bradford, Gibson Co., Tennessee

Thomas B. Crider was a physician and a farmer. He reportedly had an office in the front of his house. His granddaughter, Anita, remembered being terrified of the skeleton in his office. He was called a "Saddlebag doctor" because he made housecalls on horseback and was often gone for many days at a time. His wife managed the farm during his frequent absences and took over his practice after his death.

January 1, 1838, Thomas was named an Executor of his father's will

♥ Thomas married NANCY WARD January 19, 1843, in Gibson Co., Tennessee, daughter of WILLIS WARD and TEMPERENCE WINSLOW. Nancy was born on March 16, 1826, at Nash Co., North Carolina; died on March 8, 1904, at Bradford, Gibson Co., Tennessee; buried in March, 1904, at Antioch Cemetery, Bradford, Gibson Co., Tennessee.

Nancy Word took over her husband's medical practice after his death.

The name "Word" is interchangeable with "Ward" in this family. It is undetermined which is the original or correct spelling.

Children of THOMAS CRIDER and NANCY WARD are:

    i.   FELIX5 CRIDER, b. 1844, Bradford, Gibson Co., Tennessee.
    ii.   SAFRONIA J. CRIDER, b. 1845, Bradford, Gibson Co., Tennessee; m. W. W. THORN, January 26, 1870, Gibson Co., Tennessee.
    iii. SOPHIA CRIDER, b. 1847, Bradford, Gibson Co., Tennessee.
    iv. FOUNTAIN CRIDER, b. 1849, Bradford, Gibson Co., Tennessee.

72.   v.   JAMES WINSLOW CRIDER, b. September 25, 1851, Gibson
              Co., Tennessee; d. December 18, 1924, Bradford, Gibson Co.,
              Tennessee.
        vi.   THOMAS CRIDER, b. 1853, Bradford, Gibson Co., Tennessee.
        vii. NANCY CRIDER, b. 1856, Bradford, Gibson Co., Tennessee.
        viii. GEORGE CRIDER, b. 1857, Bradford, Gibson Co., Tennessee.
        ix.   ROBERT CRIDER, b. 1860, Bradford, Gibson Co., Tennessee.

31. SAMUEL J.4 CRIDER *(GEORGE3, DANIEL2 KRIDER, JOHN
MICHAEL1 KREIDER)* was born Abt. 1814 in Pittsylvania Co., Virginia,
and died Aft. 1860 in Weakley Co., Tennessee.

The 1850 Gibson County census lists Samuel J. Crider as having been
born in Tennessee. This is questionable as his family was living in
Virginia. The accuracy of the census depends on the census taker and
who was home to answer the questions.

The 1860 Census lists S.J. Crider and wife Mary as living in Weakley
County, Tennessee. The only children listed in this census are Robert
and Mary.

Samuel J. Crider was a minister.

♥ Samuel married MARY YATES February 28, 1835, in Gibson Co.,
Tennessee. Mary was born in 1820 in Tennessee.

Children of SAMUEL CRIDER and MARY YATES are:

        i.   JOSEPHINE5 CRIDER, b. 1836, Bradford, Gibson Co..
        ii.   ANN CRIDER, b. 1838, Bradford, Gibson Co., Tennessee.
        iii. ROBERT CRIDER, b. 1840, Bradford, Gibson Co., Tennessee.
        iv.   CALVIN CRIDER, b. 1842, Bradford, Gibson Co., Tennessee.
        v.   MARY CRIDER, b. 1845, Bradford, Gibson Co., Tennessee.

vi. THOMAS CRIDER, b. 1847, Bradford, Gibson Co., Tennessee.

32. DANIEL BENNETT4 CRIDER *(GEORGE3, DANIEL2 KRIDER, JOHN MICHAEL1 KREIDER)* was born in 1815 in Virginia, and died Aft. August 8, 1870, in Bradford, Gibson Co., Tennessee. Buried: Bradford, Gibson Co., Tennessee

D.B. Crider is listed as a mechanic in the 1850 Gibson County census.

♥ Daniel married ELIZA H. RIGSBY May 26, 1838, in Gibson Co., Tennessee. Eliza was born in 1815 in Tennessee; died after August 8, 1870, at Gibson Co., Tennessee.

The Bondsman at the marriage of Daniel B. Crider and Eliza H. Rigsby was T.B. Crider (Thomas Bennett, his brother).

Children of DANIEL CRIDER and ELIZA RIGSBY are:

  i. HIRAM N.5 CRIDER, b. 1839, Gibson Co., Tennessee; d. March 15, 1862, Corinth, Alcorn Co., Mississippi; m. JOSEPHINE FITCHIE, in Tennessee.

  H.N. Crider enlisted as a Private in Capt. O.N. Wade's Company G, 12th Tennessee Volunteers, June 1, 1861, at Jackson, Tennessee. He was present until his death March 15, 1862. At the time of his death, he was a Private in Co. G, led by Capt. Walker who wrote an affidavit regarding his death (National Archives). However, a muster roll dated May 5, 1863, near Shelbyville, Tennessee, states H.N. Crider "deserted Corinth, Mississippi." It may be that Hiram's death had been overlooked!

ii. LAYBURN CRIDER, b. 1840, Gibson Co., Tennessee; d. 1864; m. NANCY STUBBLEFIELD, in Tennessee.

Layburn (Labun) E. Crider served with his brother, Hiram, in Company G of the 12th Tennessee Volunteers. He enlisted June 1, 1861, at Jackson, Tennessee. He was present until May 5, 1863, when he was listed as "Discharged."

73.　iii. PRESTON COLUMBUS CRIDER, b. November 1843, Bradford, Gibson Co., Tennessee; d. February 1918, Bradford, Gibson Co., Tennessee.

iv. SARAH CRIDER, b. 1844, Gibson Co., Tennessee; m. A. W. SMITH, June 14, 1874, Gibson Co., Tennessee.

Sarah was also known as Sally Crider.

v. ALLIFIRE CRIDER, b. 1845, Gibson Co., Tennessee.

vi. MARY CRIDER, b. 1847, Gibson Co., Tennessee; d. Bef. June 25, 1880, Gibson Co., Tennessee; m. WILSE M. SMITH, September 22, 1870, Gibson Co., Tennessee.

Mary and Martha were twins.

vii. MARTHA CRIDER, b. 1849, Gibson Co., Tennessee; m. MENROE SMITH, Gibson Co., Tennessee.

viii. WINDFIELD L. CRIDER, b. 1853, Gibson Co., Tennessee; m. E. N. RAY, Tennessee.

ix. EMMA CRIDER, b. 1856, Gibson Co., Tennessee.

33. GEORGE W.4 CRIDER *(GEORGE3, DANIEL2 KRIDER, JOHN MICHAEL1 KREIDER)* was born Abt. 1817 in Gibson Co., Tennessee, and died in Calloway Co., Kentucky.

George W. Crider was mentioned in a suit against his father's estate. He was reportedly a "citizen of Kentucky" in 1840.

♥ George married MARY ANN SPRAT BRUSH February 7, 1842, in Henry Co., Tennessee.

Children of GEORGE CRIDER and MARY BRUSH are:

74.   i.   MILTON E.5 CRIDER, b. December 19, 1842, Calloway Co., Kentucky.
        ii.   MARGARET E. CRIDER, b. 1849, Calloway Co., Kentucky.
      iii. ROSANNA C. CRIDER, b. November 5, 1852, Calloway Co., Kentucky.
      iv. BELL CRIDER, b. June 16, 1862, Calloway Co., Kentucky; d. June 2, 1924.

34. WILLIAM AIRE4 CRIDER *(HENRY3, DANIEL2 KRIDER, JOHN MICHAEL1 KREIDER)* was born November 10, 1812, in Pittsylvania Co., Virginia, and died October 05, 1884, in Carroll Co., Tennessee. Buried: Hampton Cemetery, Carroll Co., Tennessee

♥ William married REBECCA DANIEL TUCKER December, 1835, in Carroll Co., Tennessee. Rebecca was born Oct. 3, 1812, in Wake Co., North Carolina, and died May 6, 1864, in Carroll Co., Tennessee. Buried at Hampton Cemetery, Carroll Co., Tennessee.

Children of WILLIAM CRIDER and REBECCA TUCKER are:

      i.   FRANCES E.5 CRIDER, b. October 10, 1838, Carroll Co., Tennessee; d. May 12, 1867, Carroll Co., Tennessee. Buried: Hampton Cemetery, Carroll Co., Tennessee
      ii.   MARTHA ANN CRIDER, b. October 12, 1839, Carroll Co., Tennessee; d. September 20, 1920, Carroll Co., Tennessee. Buried: Hampton Cemetery, Carroll Co., Tennessee

iii. MILTON HARRISON CRIDER, b. March 4, 1841, Carroll Co., Tennessee; d. April 16, 1930; m. MARY E. FREEMAN, January 16, 1864, Carroll Co., Tennessee.

iv. MARY E. CRIDER, b. January 18, 1843, Carroll Co., Tennessee; d. January 6, 1905, Carroll Co., Tennessee; m. JOSEPH S. BROWN, September 20, 1866, Carroll Co., Tennessee. Buried: Hampton Cemetery, Carroll Co., Tennessee.

v. HENRY CLAY CRIDER, b. September 12, 1847, Carroll Co., Tennessee; d. March 17, 1904, Gainesville, Cooke Co., Texas; m. MARY ANGELINE STEELE, Abt. 1872.

vi. GEORGE WASHINGTON CRIDER, b. June 5, 1851, Carroll Co., Tennessee; d. July 23, 1931, Carroll Co., Tennessee; m. MARY ANN GOOCH, December 14, 1881, Carroll Co., Tennessee. Buried: Hampton Cemetery, Carroll Co., Tennessee.

35. RICHARD HENRY4 CRIDER *(HENRY3, DANIEL2 KRIDER, JOHN MICHAEL1 KREIDER)* was born August 7, 1817, in Smith Co., Tennessee, and died November 12, 1903, in Carroll Co., Tennessee. Buried: Hampton Cemetery, Carroll Co., Tennessee

Richard, known to family members as "Uncle Rich," was suffering so much from "The Civil War and the Yankees" he requested to be buried in Hampton Cemetery lying north and south so that on Resurrection Day he would rise with his back to the Yankees in proper disdain!" (*The Holladay Family*, A.M. Holladay, 1983)

In August, 1885, a graphic description of Carroll County was published, probably in *The Republican* newspaper. The author was R.H. Crider. It is reproduced here in its entirety:

"Mr. R.H. Crider, who is now 68 years of age, and one of the early settlers of Carroll County, on being interviewed, gave the following narrative: My father, Henry Crider, was a native of Pittsylvania County, Virginia. His father and mother were Germans, and he first learned to speak the German language, and, though afterwards he learned to talk English, he kept, to the day of his death, a German Bible, and always preferred to read it. My mother was of Virginia birth, but of English descent. Her maiden name was Permelia Lee, daughter of John Lee, who was seven years a soldier in (the) Revolutionary War. After marriage and birth of one child, Wm. A. Crider, my father and mother moved to Smith County, Tennessee, at which place I was born, and in the year 1822 we came to Carroll County and settled on a tract of land that my father had leased from Samuel Hawkins, who then resided in Maury County, Tennessee. This was the place on which was, afterwards, situated the mill of Addison Hawkins. At that time there was no cleared land on the tract, and in fact the whole county was a howling wilderness.

"I can now call to mind but two settlements for many miles around. It seems to me that a man by the name of Montgomery was living about where John Orr now lives, and there was a small settlement somewhere about where Buena Vista now is, that we called McKee town. Huntingdon had been laid off some two years before this, but I think that there were but few people living there.

"The place at which we first settled is about seven miles southeast of Huntingdon. It was several years before anybody else came into that settlement. James Hampton and William Horton were the first, and soon Moses F. Roberts settled about where Merideth Wilson now lives, and McPete settled on the old Hawkins place two miles south of Huntingdon "The county then presented a grand appearance, such as would be well calculated now to captivate a man who might expect to till the soil for a living. The bottom land was covered with pea vines knee deep, and the soil was so loose that a horse would sink to the pastern every step. The higher or barren lands were covered with what we called barren grass, often as high as man's head, which made first-rate hay. I have often known my father to mow it and stack it up out on the commons, and I think that, as a food grass, it was fully equal to the red top of today. Where this grass was not too thick, the barrens were covered with native strawberries, which, though smaller than the cultivated varieties of the present time, were very palatable. I have sat down where all the earth seemed covered with the most delicious of these berries, in a wild or uncultivated state, and without moving, gathered as many as I could eat within arm's length. There were also, at that time, many wild plums which always matured well, and was a fruit not to despised. And in many places were acres and acres of hazel loaded with fruit. In the bottom the cane was always green. There was yearly a fine mast, and with the green waving barren grass it may readily be imagined that livestock fared well. It was no trouble to keep and raise cattle, and I can recollect when we had fourteen cows giving milk at the same time. So plentiful indeed was butter that I have known my mother to make it into soap, and a splendid article it made! It was hard to beat as a shaving soap! My father once carried 100 pounds of butter to Huntingdon for sale at one time, and was only offered two cents per pound.

"With the rude implements at hand, the soil readily yielded from ten to twelve barrels of corn per acre, and almost everything that we planted came, with but little work, in great abundance.

"All the high land about Concord Church and for miles around was known as barrens, with only now and then a chance scrubby oak to be seen; and for hundreds of yards great gangs of deer could be seen bounding playfully over nature's unclaimed domain. The country seemed to be literally alive with deer. Near where Esq. R.P. Chambers now lives I have seen as many as forty at one time.

"Bear were also quite numerous. One occasion a bear came near the house and caught a black hog, and while it was squealing my father ran with his gun and fired with a view of killing the bear but missed it and killed the hog.

"One day I saw a large panther between where Wm. Springer now lives and Concord Church.

"Wild turkeys were reasonably plentiful and groundhogs and pole cats (skunks) were very common.

"Rattlesnakes were then a terror to the settlers. My father had cleared a small field of about three acres, and Wyatt, a colored, while ploughing over it one time killed five rattlesnakes--none of which measured less than five feet in length. In those days ground mice were bad about taking up corn after it had been planted; and my father and a man by the name of Miller, that lived with us, one night went out into the field with torches to scare the mice out, and while there, the rattlesnakes commenced to rattle in every direction, and so terrorized the torch bearers as to cause them to beat a hasty retreat back to the house leaving the snakes and the mice in possession of the field.

"At this early day the opposum was the terror of the poultry yard--so much so that it was with great difficulty that chickens could be reared on account of his depredations.

"Bee trees were then plentiful and we always had honey in abundance.

"When there were but few inhabitants here the society was very good, and great hospitality prevailed among the settlers. It is true they did not have much money, nor did they need much. What they wore and what they (ate) was made at home; and of both apparel and food there was always a bountiful supply--such as it was. There were then no mills in the county, and our meal was grated or beaten in the mortar. I think that the first mill in the county was Blount's mill, on Blount Creek on the east side of Sandy River.

"About this time I was but a small boy, and my recollection, I should think, would not be so good as would that of Wilson Nesbitt, who was one of the early settlers of the county and older at the time than I was.

"There was but few roads in the country then. My father helped to cut the Lexington road after we came here. No Indians lived here, but it had been their hunting ground and I saw a number of Indian camps or shelters covered with cane and bark; and on the place where I now live was a high place or mound about which I have found javelins and old pieces of pottery.

"The country today, though exhibiting many evidences of the advance of art and science, does not present the imposing prospect for the farmers that charmed all sixty years ago. Where we then had a rich and alluvial mould, the earth is now packed and hard; and where we could then produce twelve barrels of corn to the acre we would now be glad to get six. While time has worked such a change upon the face of the country its effect is even more distinct upon the families that resided here at that time, the older members having nearly all passed away." (Ibid.)

♥ Richard married EADY BRINKLEY in January, 1837, at Carroll Co., Tennessee. Eady was born on May 18, 1819, in North Carolina; died on November 27, 1852, at Carroll Co., Tennessee; buried at Hampton Cemetery, Carroll Co., Tennessee.

Children of RICHARD CRIDER and EADY BRINKLEY are:

	i.	RICHARD H.5 CRIDER, b. 1837, Carroll Co., Tennessee; d. Abt. 1837, Carroll Co., Tennessee.
75.	ii.	FELIX HENRY CRIDER, b. October 19, 1838, Carroll Co., Tennessee; d. September 19, 1924, Carroll Co., Tennessee.
	iii.	DANIEL D. CRIDER, b. February 8, 1840, Carroll Co., Tennessee; d. July 28, 1864, Atlanta, Fulton Co., Georgia.

Daniel D. Crider died fighting in the Battle of Atlanta in the Civil War. His brother died with him.

iv. JOSEPHUS F. CRIDER, b. March 20, 1842, Carroll Co., Tennessee; d. July 28, 1864, Atlanta, Fulton Co., Georgia.

Josephus, along with his brother Daniel, died fighting in the Civil War. They died on the same day, in the Battle of Atlanta.

v. MARY CRIDER, b. July 25, 1843, Carroll Co., Tennessee; d. October 7, 1874, Carroll Co., Tennessee; m. JOSEPH S. BROWN, December 20, 1866, Carroll Co., Tennessee. Buried: Hampton Cemetery, Carroll Co., Tennessee

vi. JOHN DEWITT CLINTON CRIDER, b. March 3, 1844, Carroll Co., Tennessee; d. Abt. 1917, Carroll Co., Tennessee; buried: Hampton Cemetery, Carroll Co., Tennessee; m. WINIFRED J. LAWRENCE, December 8, 1875, Carroll Co., Tennessee.

vii. PAMELA CATHERINE CRIDER, b. 1846, Carroll Co., Tennessee; d. March 27, 1932, Gibson Co., Tennessee; m. DANIEL H. DALTON, December 23, 1867, Tennessee.

viii. ELCEBENER B. CRIDER, b. July 26, 1848, Carroll Co., Tennessee; d. August 3, 1884, Carroll Co., Tennessee; buried: Hampton Cemetery, Carroll Co., Tennessee; m. JOHN COLUMBUS HALL, December 18, 1872, Carroll Co., Tennessee.

ix. IRTY MISSY CRIDER, b. March 4, 1851, Carroll Co., Tennessee; d. August 14, 1852, Carroll Co., Tennessee; buried: Hampton Cemetery, Carroll Co., Tennessee.

x. ZIPPORA P. CRIDER, b. October 6, 1855, Carroll Co., Tennessee; d. September 26, 1899, Carroll Co., Tennessee; m. LEONIDAS HOLLADAY, November 11, 1874, Carroll Co., Tennessee; buried: Hampton Cemetery, Carroll Co., Tennessee.

xi. HATTON H. CRIDER, b. 1858, Carroll Co., Tennessee; d. November 22, 1859, Carroll Co., Tennessee; buried: Hampton Cemetery, Carroll Co., Tennessee.

36. CATHERINE4 CRIDER *(HENRY3, DANIEL2 KRIDER, JOHN MICHAEL1 KREIDER)* was born May 4, 1819, in Smith Co., Tennessee, and died October 14, 1914, in Carroll Co., Tennessee; buried: Hampton Cemetery, Carroll Co., Tennessee.

♥ Catherine married GEORGE WASHINGTON HOLLADAY July 19, 1835, in Carroll Co., Tennessee, son of DAVID HOLLADAY and ANN LEE. George was born June 18, 1811, at Jackson, Madison Co., Tennessee, and died on Apr. 18, 1865, at Carroll Co., Tennessee. He was buried at Hampton Cemetery, Carroll Co., Tennessee.

Children of CATHERINE CRIDER and GEORGE HOLLADAY are:

76.   i.   ALLEN5 HOLLADAY, b. December 5, 1851, Carroll Co., Tennessee; d. August 2, 1928, Carroll Co., Tennessee.
         ii.   LEONIDAS HOLLADAY, b. September 13, 1853, Carroll Co., Tennessee; d. November 3, 1930, Carroll Co., Tennessee; m. ZIPPORA P. CRIDER, November 11, 1874, Carroll Co., Tennessee; buried: Hampton Cemetery, Carroll Co., Tennessee

37. EMALINE4 CRIDER *(HENRY3, DANIEL2 KRIDER, JOHN MICHAEL1 KREIDER)* was born March 20, 1821, in Smith Co., Tennessee, and died November 12, 1898, in Carroll Co., Tennessee; buried: Hampton Cemetery, Carroll Co., Tennessee.

After Stephen and Emaline married, they lived in a small house near Henry Crider on Beaver Creek. Five years later, after Emaline's mother died, they bought a farm and moved about one mile south of the present Concord Primitive Baptist Church. Stephen made his living as a farmer all his life. He and his family were members of the Concord Missionary Baptist Church. (The Holladay Family, A.M. Holladay, 1983)

According to a court case filed in Chancery Court of Carroll County, May 25, 1869, by Emaline's brother, John Daniel Crider, Stephen and Emaline received many wedding presents from her father, Henry. These included one filly (mare), one cow and calf, one sow and pigs, some sheep, one feather bed and bedstead and "suitable bed clothing to set off a bed," and one loom, one large chest, some chairs, one wash pot, set of knives and forks, plates and cups. He also gave them a slave boy named Hard, age 8 or 10, as well as girl named Perliney. John Daniel Crider was protesting that the boy, Hard, had been willed to the children of Henry Crider, and that Emaline's use of him for nine years was worth, with interest, $733.00.

♥ Emaline married STEPHEN CARROLL HOLLADAY January 23, 1844, in Carroll Co., Tennessee, son of DAVID HOLLADAY and ANN LEE. Stephen was born June 4, 1816, at Smith Co., Tennessee, and died June 24, 1887, at Carroll Co., Tennessee. Stephen was buried at Hampton Cemetery, Carroll Co., Tennessee.

Stephen was named for his father's brother, Stephen, and for Gen. William Carroll under whom his father served in War of 1812.

Stephen moved to Carroll County about 1832. He probably continued his schooling in his new home.

Children of EMALINE CRIDER and STEPHEN HOLLADAY are:

- i.   LEONIDAS5 HOLLADAY, b. January 30, 1845, Carroll Co., Tennessee; d. January 27, 1850, Carroll Co., Tennessee.
- ii.   WILLIAM ANDREW HOLLADAY, b. December 9, 1846, Carroll Co., Tennessee; d. October 9, 1921.
- iii. VERONA E. HOLLADAY, b. August 22, 1848, Carroll Co., Tennessee; d. July 1890.
- iv.   MARTIN LUTHER HOLLADAY, b. October 22, 1849, Carroll Co., Tennessee; d. December 9, 1923.
- v.   AMANDA CALEDONIA HOLLADAY, b. January 24, 1851, Carroll Co., Tennessee; d. August 16, 1916.
- vi.   PEORIA ANN HOLLADAY, b. October 22, 1853, Carroll Co., Tennessee; d. March 28, 1928.
- vii. LEONIA CATHERINE HOLLADAY, b. June 15, 1855, Carroll Co., Tennessee; d. November 4, 1926.

viii. MAJOR GILBERT HOLLADAY, b. December 9, 1857, Carroll Co., Tennessee; d. July 20, 1908.

ix. SAMUEL HOUSTON HOLLADAY, b. February 18, 1859, Carroll Co., Tennessee; d. June 19, 1927.

x. STEPHEN LEE HOLLADAY, b. January 18, 1864, Carroll Co., Tennessee; d. July 18, 1936.

38. JAMES CARROLL4 CRIDER *(HENRY3, DANIEL2 KRIDER, JOHN MICHAEL1 KREIDER)* was born March 11, 1824, in Carroll Co., Tennessee, and died Abt. 1895 in Carroll Co., Tennessee. Buried: Hampton Cemetery, Carroll Co., Tennessee

♥ James married (1) JANE E. WEATHERS February 13, 1845, in Carroll Co., Tennessee. Jane was born in 1827 in Wake Co., North Carolina; and died in 1860 at Carroll Co., Tennessee. She was buried at Hampton Cemetery, Carroll Co., Tennessee.

Children of JAMES CRIDER and JANE WEATHERS are:

vii. BEATRICE5 CRIDER, b. June 22, 1846, Carroll Co., Tennessee; d. November 9, 1912, Carroll Co., Tennessee; m. ELI DANIEL BROWN, November 9, 1862, Carroll Co., Tennessee. Buried: Hampton Cemetery, Carroll Co., Tennessee

viii. PERMELIA A. E. CRIDER, b. 1847, Carroll Co., Tennessee; d. February 22, 1925, Hickman Co., Kentucky; m. LEWIS A. MARTIN, September 24, 1873, Carroll Co., Tennessee. Buried: Poplar Grove Cem, Hickman Co., Kentucky

ix. TIERACY SUSAN CRIDER, b. August 8, 1848, Carroll Co., Tennessee; d. January 14, 1905, Carroll Co., Tennessee; m. W. E. "BUD" SELLERS, December 27, 1882, Carroll Co., Tennessee. Buried: Hampton Cemetery, Carroll Co., Tennessee

x. JOHN BELL CRIDER, b. 1854, Carroll Co., Tennessee; d. Abt. 1880, Carroll Co., Tennessee; m. MARTHA OATSVALL, February 20, 1877, Carroll Co., Tennessee. Buried: Hampton Cemetery, Carroll Co., Tennessee

xi. THEODOSIA CRIDER, b. 1856, Carroll Co., Tennessee.
xii. MARTHA J. CRIDER, b. 1858, Carroll Co., Tennessee; d. Abt. 1912, Carroll Co., Tennessee; m. J. HARRISON ROARK, August 30, 1882, Carroll Co., Tennessee.

❤ James married (2) JACKIE OATSVALL MCCLAIN after 1860. She was buried in Hampton Cemetery, Carroll Co., Tennessee

Children of JAMES CRIDER and JACKIE MCCLAIN are:

i. ELSA ELMIRA5 CRIDER, b. February 9, 1864, Carroll Co., Tennessee; d. December 3, 1940, Gibson Co., Tennessee; m. WILLIAM B. BRANDON, December 8, 1881, Carroll Co., Tennessee.
ii. JAMES A. CRIDER, b. 1866, Carroll Co., Tennessee; d. Gibson Co., Tennessee; m. SARAH A. HOLT, February 12, 1890, Gibson Co., Tennessee.
77. iii. ROBERT MONROE CRIDER, b. 1868, Carroll Co., Tennessee; d. January 27, 1931, Carroll Co., Tennessee.
iv. EUGENIA FRANCES CRIDER, b. March 19, 1869, Carroll Co., Tennessee; d. August 1, 1943, Hickman Co., Kentucky; m. JAMES MORRIS, Abt. 1897, Tennessee. Buried: Poplar Grove Cem, Hickman Co., Kentucky
v. GEORGIA ETHEL CRIDER, b. May 8, 1876, Carroll Co., Tennessee; d. June 12, 1958, Gibson Co., Tennessee; m. FREEMAN KEMP, November 11, 1881, Tennessee.
vi. DUDLEY T. CRIDER, b. Abt. 1878, Carroll Co., Tennessee; d. Michigan; m. BELLE ROSS, January 16, 1901, Tennessee.

39. JOHN DANIEL4 CRIDER *(HENRY3, DANIEL2 KRIDER, JOHN MICHAEL1 KREIDER)* was born February 15, 1826,in Carroll Co., Tennessee, and died August 31, 1904, in Carroll Co., Tennessee. Buried: Hampton Cemetery, Carroll Co., Tennessee

♥ John married MARTHA WEATHERS September 5, 1850, in Carroll Co., Tennessee. Martha was born in 1827 in Wake Co., North Carolina, and died in 1861 at Carroll Co., Tennessee. Buried at Hampton Cemetery, Carroll Co., Tennessee

Children of JOHN CRIDER and MARTHA WEATHERS are:

    i.   EUSTIAN RANDOLPH5 CRIDER, b. July 19, 1853, Carroll Co., Tennessee; d. October 30, 1934, Texas.

    ii. NANCY HATTIE CRIDER, b. June 23, 1857, Carroll Co., Tennessee; d. October 18, 1935, Carroll Co., Tennessee; m. MESSER NORTON OATSVALL, February 20, 1875, Carroll Co., Tennessee. Buried: Hampton Cemetery, Carroll Co., Tennessee.

    iii. MARTHA POPE CRIDER, b. July 1860, Carroll Co., Tennessee; d. Abt. 1860, Carroll Co., Tennessee.

    iv. EDNA CRIDER, b. November 28, 1865, Carroll Co., Tennessee; d. January 25, 1873, Carroll Co., Tennessee. Buried: Hampton Cemetery, Carroll Co., Tennessee

    v. FRANCES EMMA CRIDER, b. December 24, 1867, Carroll Co., Tennessee; d. 1953, Carroll Co., Tennessee; m. JOHN WORRELL, August 28, 1886, Carroll Co., Tennessee. Buried: Hampton Cemetery, Carroll Co., Tennessee

    vi. DELANO C. CRIDER, b. 1868, Carroll Co., Tennessee; d. Abt. 1868, Carroll Co., Tennessee. Buried: Hampton Cemetery, Carroll Co., Tennessee

    vii. LULU CRIDER, b. February 5, 1870, Carroll Co., Tennessee; d. October 1890, Carroll Co., Tennessee; m. EBB CHAMBERS, September 3, 1889, Carroll Co., Tennessee. Buried: Hampton Cemetery, Carroll Co., Tennessee.

    viii. JOSEPH WALTER CRIDER, b. March 3, 1872, Carroll Co., Tennessee; d. November 19, 1955, Texas; m. LYDIA ARIZONA ROBERTS, Abt. 1901, Carroll Co., Tennessee.

    ix. MEXIE CRIDER, b. April 30, 1874, Carroll Co., Tennessee; d. January 23, 1950, Carroll Co., Tennessee; m. BENNIE CHAMBERS, April 20, 1892, Carroll Co., Tennessee.

Buried: Hampton Cemetery, Carroll Co., Tennessee
   x.   NEVIA CRIDER, b. September 25, 1876, Carroll Co.,
       Tennessee; d. October 16, 1907, Carroll Co., Tennessee.
       Buried: Hampton Cemetery, Carroll Co., Tennessee
  xi. VELLIE CRIDER, b. January 6, 1880, Carroll Co., Tennessee;
       d. June 13, 1951, Carroll Co., Tennessee; m. EUGENE ORR,
       January 25, 1902, Carroll Co., Tennessee.

40. ANDREW JACKSON4 CRIDER *(HENRY3, DANIEL2 KRIDER, JOHN MICHAEL1 KREIDER)* was born September 24, 1829, in Carroll Co., Tennessee, and died June 01, 1906, in Hempstead Co., Arkansas. Buried: Hope, Hempstead Co., Arkansas

♥ Andrew married ARTILL HAMPTON June 16, 1853, in Carroll Co., Tennessee. Artill was born in 1828 in Carroll Co., Tennessee, and died Sept. 30, 1902, at Hempstead Co., Arkansas.

Children of ANDREW CRIDER and ARTILL HAMPTON are:

    i.   VICTORIA ANN5 CRIDER, b. November 12, 1855, Carroll Co.,
       Tennessee; d. 1925, Texarkana, Miller Co., Arkansas; m.
       WILLIAM TRAVIS BOWDEN, Abt. 1875, Arkansas.
   ii. JAMES HENRY CRIDER, b. February 12, 1857, Carroll Co.,
       Tennessee; d. May 17, 1908, Arkansas; m. MATTIE
       LANGSTON, 1892, Arkansas.
  iii. PERMELIA JANE CRIDER, b. 1864, Carroll Co., Tennessee; d.
       Arkansas.

41. DANIEL W.4 CRIDER *(SAMUEL3, DANIEL2 KRIDER, JOHN MICHAEL1 KREIDER)* was born February 27, 1809, in Pittsylvania Co., Virginia, and died April 25, 1839, in Livingston Co., Kentucky.

Daniel wrote his will April 23, 1839, in Livingston County (Will Book B). He mentioned father, Samuel Crider, Bryant W. Bennett, Jacob Green, and William H. Crider, any of them to be executors. He ordered his land sold, and one-third of the proceeds were to go to daughter, Araminta, child of his first marriage. One half was to go to "...present wife, Lilly Ann, and her son Allen (from her first marriage), equally, and a horse if she wants it." The remainder was to pay for Araminta's education. Step-son Allen "...will be cared for by his mother as well as I can tell her." The witnesses were Jacob Green and Samuel Crider, who were also executors. The will was proven May 6, 1839.

♥ Daniel married MARY MCELROY April 25, 1829, in Livingston Co., Kentucky.

Child of DANIEL CRIDER and MARY MCELROY is:

78.   i.   ARAMINTA5 CRIDER, b. August 22, 1833, Kentucky; d. January 16, 1852, Kentucky.

42. FINIS EWING4 CRIDER *(SAMUEL3, DANIEL2 KRIDER, JOHN MICHAEL1 KREIDER)* was born December 1, 1818, in Livingston Co., Kentucky, and died January 21, 1881, in Jefferson Co., Illinois. Buried: Thurmond Cem., Jefferson Co., Illinois

Finis and family moved to Jefferson County, Illinois, in 1866 (Thelma Clinton Whittington, *History and Families of Livingston County, Kentucky*).

♥ Finis married SARAH TOWREY in Kentucky. Sarah was the daughter of Edward and Margaret McDowell Towery. Born in 1821 in Caldwell

Co., Kentucky, Sarah died in 1886 in Jefferson Co., Illinois. Buried: Thurmond Cem., Jefferson Co., Illinois

Children of FINIS CRIDER and SARAH TOWREY are:

    i.   MARGARET A.5 CRIDER, b. 1841, Caldwell Co., Kentucky; m. J. D. MORSE, November 17, 1861, Caldwell Co., Kentucky.

          The International Genealogical Index shows two Margaret A. Criders marrying in Caldwell County on the same date. The spouses are shown as J.D. Morse and Balas Morse. The original records have not been examined to decipher if there were two couples or a misreading of the record.

    ii. GEORGE W. CRIDER, b. 1847, Caldwell Co., Kentucky.
   iii. WILLIAM T. CRIDER, b. September 1, 1852, Caldwell Co., Kentucky.
   iv. LEWIS CASS CRIDER, b. July 23, 1856, Caldwell Co., Kentucky.
    v. SARAH CRIDER, b. March 1860, Caldwell Co., Kentucky.
   vi. MARY M. CRIDER, b. November 20, 1861, Caldwell Co., Kentucky.

43. WILLIAM H.4 CRIDER *(SAMUEL3, DANIEL2 KRIDER, JOHN MICHAEL1 KREIDER)* was born Abt. 1819 in Livingston Co., Kentucky.

♥ William married MATILDA MCELROY April 9, 1837, in Livingston Co., Kentucky.

Child of WILLIAM CRIDER and MATILDA MCELROY is:

    i.   OLIVIA5 CRIDER, b. 1848, Crittenden Co., Kentucky.

44. SAMUEL F.4 CRIDER *(SAMUEL3, DANIEL2 KRIDER, JOHN MICHAEL1 KREIDER)* was born Abt. 1828 in Livingston Co., Kentucky, and died September 10, 1856, in Crittenden Co., Kentucky.

♥ Samuel married MARY SALINA CRIDER March 30, 1848, in Crittenden Co., Kentucky, daughter of SAMUEL CRIDER and POLLY FOSTER. Mary was born in 1830 in Livingston Co., Kentucky.

Children of SAMUEL CRIDER and MARY CRIDER are:

     i.   MARY J.5 CRIDER, b. 1849, Crittenden Co., Kentucky.
    ii. E. A. CRIDER, b. 1850, Crittenden Co., Kentucky.

45. MELISSA ELIZABETH4 CRIDER *(WILLIAM B.3, DANIEL2 KRIDER, JOHN MICHAEL1 KREIDER)* was born February 28, 1826, in Pittsylvania Co., Virginia, and died Bef. June, 1864, in Pittsylvania Co., Virginia.

Melissa was deceased by June 23,1864, when her father, William, mentioned her in his will.

♥ Melissa married WILLIAM GREGORY April 15, 1844, in Pittsylvania Co., Virginia.

Children of MELISSA CRIDER and WILLIAM GREGORY are:

     i.   CAROLINE5 GREGORY, b. Abt. 1846, Pittsylvania Co., Virginia.
    ii. ANGELINE GREGORY, b. Abt. 1848, Pittsylvania Co., Virginia.

46. SUSAN C.4 CRIDER *(WILLIAM B.3, DANIEL2 KRIDER, JOHN MICHAEL1 KREIDER)* was born in 1836 in Pittsylvania Co., Virginia.

♥ Susan married JAMES MOODY SHELHORSE June 11, 1857, in Pittsylvania Co., Virginia.

Child of SUSAN CRIDER and JAMES SHELHORSE is:

79.   i.   SUSAN B.5 SHELHORSE, b. 1863, Pittsylvania Co., Virginia; d. Abt. 1887, Pittsylvania Co., Virginia.

FIFTH GENERATION

47. JACOB5 GREEN *(MARY POLLY4 CRIDER, JACOB3, DANIEL2 KRIDER, JOHN MICHAEL1 KREIDER)* was born November 13, 1817, in Pittsylvania Co., Virginia, and died September 1, 1837, in Crittenden Co., Kentucky.

♥ Jacob married ELIZABETH BENNETT September 10, 1837, in Livingston Co., Kentucky. Elizabeth was born Feb 11, 1821, and died July 15, 1856, in Crittenden Co., Kentucky.

Children of JACOB GREEN and ELIZABETH BENNETT are:

     i.   FRANKLIN6 GREEN, b. September 10, 1838, Kentucky; d. October 31, 1839.

    ii.   WILLIAM H. GREEN, b. October 31, 1839, Kentucky.

   iii.   DAVID B. GREEN, b. April 21, 1841, Kentucky.

   iv.   GEORGE B. GREEN, b. May 19, 1843, Kentucky; d. October 14, 1843, Kentucky.

    v.   GEORGE C. GREEN, b. August 12, 1844, Kentucky; d. August 25, 1844, Kentucky.

   vi.   SARAH E. GREEN, b. March 4, 1846, Kentucky; d. Dec. 1, 1873, Kentucky.

  vii.   MARY ANN GREEN, b. October 26, 1847, Kentucky; d. August 18, 1934.

 viii.   LUCY JANE GREEN, b. September 1, 1849, Kentucky; d. June 10, 1850, Kentucky.

   ix.   CHARLOTTE H. GREEN, b. January 27, 1852, Kentucky; d. April 22, 1944.

    x.   NANCY SUSAN GREEN, b. July 3, 1853, Kentucky.

   xi.   JACOB M. GREEN, b. March 14, 1856, Kentucky; d. October 5, 1856, Kentucky.

48. JOHN HENRY5 CRIDER *(HENRY4, DANIEL3, DANIEL2 KRIDER, JOHN MICHAEL1 KREIDER)* was born November 12, 1819, in Livingston Co., Kentucky, and died September 29, 1851, in Crittenden Co., Kentucky. Buried: Piney Fork Cem., Crittenden Co., Kentucky

♥ John married LEWRANEY HUGHEY October 10, 1838, in Livingston Co., Kentucky, daughter of ALLEN HUGHEY and SARAH WAGGONER. She was born Mar. 3, 1817, in Livingston Co., Kentucky, and died Apr. 26, 1896, in Caldwell Co., Kentucky. She was buried at Pleasant Hill Cemetery, Caldwell Co., Kentucky.

Children of JOHN CRIDER and LEWRANEY HUGHEY are:

80.   i.   ALLEN TOM6 CRIDER, b. November 30, 1839, Livingston Co., Kentucky, KY; d. November 24, 1866.
81.   ii.   JASPER GROOMS CRIDER, b. August 23, 1841, Livingston Co., Kentucky; d. September 25, 1908.
     iii.   FRANCIS IRVIN CRIDER, b. August 10, 1843, Crittenden Count, KY; d. May 18, 1917.
     iv.   LOUISA M. CRIDER, b. October 1, 1845, Crittenden Count, KY; d. March 14, 1925.
     v.   CYNTHIA ADELINE CRIDER, b. November 21, 1847, Crittenden Co., Kentucky; d. December 25, 1871; m. FELIX BLACK CANNON, 1870, Princeton, Caldwell Co., Kentucky.
     vi.   MARY ANN CRIDER, b. January 23, 1850, Crittenden Co., Kentucky; d. April 27, 1905.
82.   vii.   WILLIAM H. CRIDER, b. November 29, 1851, Crittenden Co., Kentucky; d. January 7, 1935, Phillips Co., Kansas.
     viii.   SARAH ELIZABETH CRIDER, b. Abt. 1853.

49. ELIZABETH5 CRIDER *(HENRY4, DANIEL3, DANIEL2 KRIDER, JOHN MICHAEL1 KREIDER)* was born in 1821 in Livingston Co., Kentucky, and died Abt. 1847 in Crittenden Co., Kentucky.

♥ Elizabeth married JOHN AARONS March 1838 in Livingston Co., Kentucky.

Child of ELIZABETH CRIDER and JOHN AARONS is:

    i.   MARY CRIDER6 AARONS, b. 1846, Crittenden Co., Kentucky.

        Mary C. Aarons, age 14, was living in the household of her uncle William B. Crider and family in the 1860 census.

50. NANCY5 CRIDER *(HENRY4, DANIEL3, DANIEL2 KRIDER, JOHN MICHAEL1 KREIDER)* was born Abt. 1825 in Livingston Co., Kentucky, and died Bef. 1860.

♥ Nancy married JOHN AARONS February 14, 1848, in Crittenden Co., Kentucky. Was this the same man who married her older sister?

Child of NANCY CRIDER and JOHN AARONS is:

    i.   JAMES T.6 AARONS, b. 1849, Crittenden Co., Kentucky.

        James T. Aarons, age 4, was living in the home of his uncle, William B. Crider, in the 1860 census.

51. WILLIAM BENNETT5 CRIDER *(HENRY4, DANIEL3, DANIEL2 KRIDER, JOHN MICHAEL1 KREIDER)* was born April 10, 1828, in Livingston Co., Kentucky, and died October 26, 1910, in Crittenden Co., Kentucky. Buried: Piney Fork Cem., Crittenden Co., Kentucky

♥ William married (1) ARAMINTA CRIDER September 3, 1849, in Livingston Co., Kentucky, daughter of DANIEL CRIDER and MARY McELROY.

Araminta died in childbirth. Her son was born dead..

Child of WILLIAM CRIDER and ARAMINTA CRIDER is:

     i. BABY BOY6 CRIDER, b. January 15, 1852, Livingston Co., Kentucky; d. January 15, 1852, Livingston Co., Kentucky.

       This child was still-born.

♥ William married (2) ELIZABETH JANE BUTLER November 30, 1852, in Kentucky. Buried: Piney Fork Cem., Crittenden Co., Kentucky

Child of WILLIAM CRIDER and ELIZABETH BUTLER is:

     ii. MAGNOLIA6 CRIDER, b. March 10, 1874, Crittenden Co., Kentucky.

52. RACHEL T.5 CRIDER *(HENRY4, DANIEL3, DANIEL2 KRIDER, JOHN MICHAEL1 KREIDER)* was born November 19, 1831, in Livingston Co., Kentucky, and died March 27, 1859, in Crittenden Co., Kentucky. Buried: Piney Fork Cem., Crittenden Co., Kentucky

♥ Rachel married JACOB JAMES August 02, 1847, in Crittenden Co., Kentucky, son of WILLIAM JAMES and ELIZABETH CRIDER. Jacob was born Dec. 2, 1825, in Crittenden Co., Kentucky, and died Apr. 26, 1906, in Kentucky. He was buried in Piney Fork Cem., Crittenden Co., Kentucky.

Children of RACHEL CRIDER and JACOB JAMES are:

    i.   JASPER N.6 JAMES, b. April 12, 1848, Crittenden Co., Kentucky; d. August 20, 1850.
    ii.   HENRY H. JAMES, b. January 13, 1850, Crittenden Co., Kentucky; d. January 13, 1850, Crittenden Co., Kentucky.
   iii. MARY J. JAMES, b. Abt. 1852, Crittenden Co., Kentucky.
   iv. JOHN R. JAMES, b. November 22, 1854, Crittenden Co., Kentucky; d. November 21, 1855, Crittenden Co., Kentucky.

53. JACOB5 JAMES *(ELIZABETH BETSY4 CRIDER, JACOB3, DANIEL2 KRIDER, JOHN MICHAEL1 KREIDER)* was born December 2, 1825, in Crittenden Co., Kentucky, and died April 26, 1906, in Kentucky, Kentucky. Buried: Piney Fork Cem., Crittenden Co., Kentucky

♥ Jacob married his cousin (1) RACHEL T. CRIDER August 2, 1847 in Crittenden Co., Kentucky, daughter of HENRY CRIDER and CATHERINE CRIDER (see above).

Children of JACOB JAMES and RACHEL CRIDER are:

    i.   JASPER N.6 JAMES, b. April 12, 1848, Crittenden Co., Kentucky; d. August 20, 1850.
    ii.   HENRY H. JAMES, b. January 13, 1850, Crittenden Co., Kentucky; d. January 13, 1850, Crittenden Co., Kentucky.
   iii. MARY J. JAMES, b. Abt. 1852, Crittenden Co., Kentucky.
   iv. JOHN R. JAMES, b. November 22, 1854, Crittenden Co.,

♥ Jacob married (2) LEWRANEY HUGHEY Aft. 1859 in Crittenden Co., Kentucky, daughter of ALLEN HUGHEY and SARAH WAGGONER. (see above).

Child of JACOB JAMES and LEWRANEY HUGHEY is:

v. SARAH ELIZABETH6 JAMES, b. October 6, 1860, Crittenden
    Co., Kentucky; m. THOMAS LEANDER WALKER, February 20,
    1877, Crittenden Co., Kentucky.

54. JACOB EWING5 CRIDER *(JACOB B.*4, *JACOB*3, *DANIEL*2 *KRIDER,*
*JOHN MICHAEL*1 *KREIDER)* was born May 25, 1842, in Princeton,
Caldwell Co., Kentucky, and died 1927 in Caldwell Co., Kentucky.
Buried: 1927, Fredonia Cem., Caldwell Co., Kentucky.

Jacob attended Cumberland Presbyterian College in Princeton,
Caldwell County. He was overseer on his father's farm at the age of
eighteen. In later years, he owned 600 acres of land. From 1885 to 1886
he served as a Representative from Caldwell County in the state
legislature.

♥ Jacob married ALICE WYATT 1867 in Caldwell Co., Kentucky.
Alice was the daughter of FRANKLIN D. WYATT and ELIZABETH
C. RICE. Buried: 1921, Fredonia Cem., Caldwell Co., Kentucky

Children of JACOB CRIDER and ALICE WYATT are:

	i.	NELLIE6 CRIDER, b. 1868, Caldwell Co., Kentucky; d. 1930.
83.	ii.	ZACHARIAH JOHNSON CRIDER, b. 1871, Caldwell Co., Kentucky; d. 1932, Caldwell Co., Kentucky.
	iii.	HERBERT LEE CRIDER, b. 1873, Caldwell Co., Kentucky; d. 1876, Caldwell Co., Kentucky.
84.	iv.	JACOB EWING CRIDER , JR., b. 1880, Caldwell Co., Kentucky; d. 1950, Caldwell Co., Kentucky.

55. MARY SALINA5 CRIDER *(SAMUEL J.4, JACOB3, DANIEL2 KRIDER, JOHN MICHAEL1 KREIDER)* was born in 1830 in Livingston Co., Kentucky.

♥ Mary married her cousin SAMUEL F. CRIDER March 30, 1848, in Crittenden Co., Kentucky, son of SAMUEL CRIDER and MARY DEBOE.

Children of MARY CRIDER and SAMUEL CRIDER are:

      i.   MARY J.6 CRIDER, b. 1849, Crittenden Co., Kentucky.
     ii.   E. A. CRIDER, b. 1850, Crittenden Co., Kentucky.

56. PRESLEY HARRIS5 CRIDER *(WILLIAM M.4, JACOB3, DANIEL2 KRIDER, JOHN MICHAEL1 KREIDER)* was born Abt. 1830 in Livingston Co., Kentucky.

♥ Presley married SARAH ANN PHILLIPS January 1, 1856, in Crittenden Co., Kentucky.

Presley and Sarah were married at the home of Samuel Crider by J.H. Nichol. The witnesses were D.B. Stephenson and J.M. Dean. Sarah's surname is given by some sources as Phillips.

Child of PRESLEY CRIDER and SARAH PHILLIPS is:

      i.   GEORGE M.6 CRIDER, b. July 25, 1861, Crittenden Co., Kentucky; d. April 5, 1917.

57. WILLIAM BRADLEY5 CRIDER *(WILLIAM M.*4, *JACOB*3, *DANIEL*2 *KRIDER, JOHN MICHAEL*1 *KREIDER)* was born January 20, 1831, in Livingston Co., Kentucky, and died in 1883 in Crittenden Co., Kentucky. Buried at Chapel Hill Cemetery, Crittenden Co., Kentucky

The following items appeared in the *Marion Reporter* (newspaper), Crittenden County, Kentucky.

August 11, 1880: "Bradley Crider (and others) are preparing to make an overland journey to Arkansas and return. They propose to spend six weeks making the round trip."

February 16, 1881 "George Crider left for Missouri Monday. His father, Bradley Crider, will emigrate to that state in March.

March 3, 1881 "Mr. George Crider, who left two weeks ago for Missouri and to prepare a home for his father and family, returned to Marion Saturday. He is satisfied Kentucky will be a better home."

♥ William married MARTHA JANE ADAMS Bef. 1859 in Kentucky. Martha was born Dec. 11, 1839, at Springfield, Tennessee. She died Nov. 3, 1902 in Crittenden Co., Kentucky, and is buried at Chapel Hill Cemetery, Crittenden Co., Kentucky.

Children of WILLIAM CRIDER and MARTHA ADAMS are:

85.   i.   MARY MELISSA6 CRIDER, b. September 23, 1859, Cochran Hill, Crittenden Co., Kentucky; d. 1938, Marion, Crittenden Co., Kentucky.

86.   ii. GEORGE HARRIS CRIDER, b. March 7, 1862, Marion, Crittenden Co., Kentucky.

       iii. JOSEPH HENRY CRIDER, b. 1864, Kentucky; d. 1867, Kentucky.

       iv. SARAH MARGARET CRIDER, b. July 2, 1867, Cochran Hill, Crittenden Co., Kentucky; d. September 3, 1953, Marion,

Crittenden Co., Kentucky; buried: September 5, 1953, Marion, Crittenden Co., Kentucky m. JOHN BOB HINA, February 20, 1912, Chapel Hill, Crittenden Co., Kentucky. He was buried: August 22, 1935, at Bells Mines, Crittenden Co., Kentucky.

Sallie was buried in Marion, unlike her husband, although her name is inscribed on his monument in Bells Mines.

Even though John and Sarah were childless, John cared for several orphaned boys, clothes, fed and educated them. One of them, John May, was his "adopted son" when he died.

John was ordained an Elder of the Bells Mines Cumberland Presbyterian Church on January 19, 1919, and served his church until his death.

87.   v.   MILTON BIRD CRIDER, b. July 9, 1870, Marion, Crittenden Co., Kentucky; d. March 19, 1920, Marshall, Saline Co., Missouri.

88.   vi.   ALBERT FOSTER CRIDER, b. January 13, 1873, Marion, Crittenden Co., Kentucky; d. September 9, 1945, Shreveport, Caddo Co., Louisiana.

89.   vii.   LAWRENCE EDWIN CRIDER, b. July 10, 1875, Marion, Crittenden Co., Kentucky; d. August 6, 1942, Marion, Crittenden Co., Kentucky.

90.   viii.   JACOB HUGHEY CRIDER, b. December 19, 1877, Marion, Crittenden Co., Kentucky; d. April 3, 1952, Marion, Crittenden Co., Kentucky.

58. SAMUEL FOSTER5 CRIDER *(WILLIAM M.4, JACOB3, DANIEL2 KRIDER, JOHN MICHAEL1 KREIDER)* was born August 16, 1832, in Livingston Co., Kentucky, and died November 22, 1894, in Crittenden Co., Kentucky.

Samuel Foster Crider wrote his will Sept. 2, 1856, in Crittenden County. He mentioned only wife Mary S.. The executors were Mary S. Crider and A.D. Crider. The witnesses were W.B. Travis, J.S.G. Green, and F.E. (Finis Ewing) Crider. The will was probated Oct. 4, 1856.

♥   Samuel married MARY ANN GUESS December 10, 1850, in Princeton, Caldwell Co., Kentucky. She was born Dec. 5, 1837 in Kentucky.

Children of SAMUEL CRIDER and MARY GUESS are:

     i.   PRESLEY DAVIS6 CRIDER, b. Abt. 1852, Crittenden Co., Kentucky; d. Abt. 1852, Crittenden Co., Kentucky.

           Presley died in infancy.

     ii. WILLIAM P. CRIDER, b. Abt. 1868, Crittenden Co., Kentucky.

59. SERENA ADALINE5 CRIDER *(WILLIAM M.4, JACOB3, DANIEL2 KRIDER, JOHN MICHAEL1 KREIDER)* was born April 3, 1834, in Livingston Co., Kentucky, and died July 16, 1879, in Crittenden Co., Kentucky.

♥   Serena married WILLIAM S. FORD October 4, 1853, in Crittenden Co., Kentucky. William was born in 1832 in Kentucky and died Oct. 11, 1878.

Sarena (sic) A. Crider and William S. Ford were married at William Crider's home (her grandfather) by W.C. Love, Minister of the Gospel. The bondsman was William B. Crider. The witnesses were William Crider and William B. Crider. The groom was 20, born in Caldwell County. The bride was 18, born in Crittenden County.

Children of SERENA CRIDER and WILLIAM FORD are:

    i.   FRANCIS M.6 FORD, b. May 29, 1855, Crittenden Co.,
         Kentucky; d. January 31, 1883, Crittenden Co., Kentucky.
   ii.   MARY P. FORD, b. Abt. 1861, Crittenden Co., Kentucky.
  iii.   RUFUS J. FORD, b. Abt. 1865, Crittenden Co., Kentucky.

60. CYNTHIA EMMELINE5 CRIDER *(WILLIAM M.*4, *JACOB*3, *DANIEL*2 *KRIDER, JOHN MICHAEL*1 *KREIDER)* was born February 21, 1836, in Livingston Co., Kentucky, and died February 17, 1866.

Emmeline died giving birth to her last child whose name and sex are unknown (Heritage of Crittenden County, Kentucky, Submitted by Fay Carol Crider, p. 88).

♥ Emmeline married ISRAEL M. BEABOUT September 20, 1854, in Crittenden Co., Kentucky. He was born Apr. 24, 1832, in Kentucky and died Oct. 29, 1900.

Children of EMMELINE CRIDER and ISRAEL BEABOUT are:

    i.   MARY A.6 BEABOUT, b. Abt. 1856, Crittenden Co., Kentucky.
   ii.   NANCY L. BEABOUT, b. Abt. 1858, Crittenden Co., Kentucky.
  iii.   ELIZABETH E. BEABOUT, b. Abt. 1860, Crittenden Co.,
         Kentucky.
  iv.   WILLIAM GRANT BEABOUT, b. Abt. 1862, Crittenden Co.,
         Kentucky.
   v.   ISRAEL FRANK BEABOUT, b. Abt. 1864, Crittenden Co.,
         Kentucky.

61. MARY JANE5 CRIDER *(WILLIAM M.4, JACOB3, DANIEL2 KRIDER, JOHN MICHAEL1 KREIDER)* was born Abt. 1840 in Livingston Co., Kentucky.

♥ Mary Jane married MATTHEW ASBURY CHADWICK August 20, 1854, in Crittenden Co., Kentucky.

Mary and Matthew left the area and may have moved to Missouri.

Children of MARY CRIDER and MATTHEW CHADWICK are:

    i. WILLIAM M.6 CHADWICK, b. Abt. 1856.
    ii. MARTHA CHADWICK, b. Abt. 1858.
    iii. JOHN P. CHADWICK, b. Abt. 1860.
    iv. CHARLES B. CHADWICK, b. Abt. 1862.
    v. JAMES H. CHADWICK, b. Abt. 1864.
    vi. DELA A. CHADWICK, b. Abt. 1866.

62. AMISON ALONZO5 CRIDER *(WILLIAM M.4, JACOB3, DANIEL2 KRIDER, JOHN MICHAEL1 KREIDER)* was born December 4, 1849, in Crittenden Co., Kentucky, and died September 28, 1891.

♥ Amison married LAURA B. THOMASON November 13, 1873 in Crittenden Co., Kentucky. Laura was born Jan. 12, 1859, in Crittenden Co., Kentucky, and died July 18, 1893.

Children of AMISON CRIDER and LAURA THOMASON are:

    i. AGGIE6 CRIDER, b. April 06, 1882, Crittenden Co., Kentucky; d. April 18, 1882, Crittenden Co., Kentucky.
    ii. MINNIE WILLIAMS CRIDER, b. July 4, 1883, Crittenden Co., Kentucky.

iii. MAUDE HENRY CRIDER, b. June 24, 1886, Crittenden Co., Kentucky; d. February 3, 1963, Crittenden Co., Kentucky; m. HULETT H. GUESS, Crittenden Co., Kentucky.
iv. ELBERT ALONZO CRIDER, b. September 1, 1889, Crittenden Co., Kentucky; d. August 6, 1961, Crittenden Co., Kentucky; m. EULA M. PARIS, Crittenden Co., Kentucky.

63. DAVIS EWING5 CRIDER *(WILLIAM M.4, JACOB3, DANIEL2 KRIDER, JOHN MICHAEL1 KREIDER)* was born July 25, 1855, in Crittenden Co., Kentucky, and died February 8, 1924, in Marion, Crittenden Co., Kentucky. Buried: Crayne Cemetery, Marion, Crittenden Co., Kentucky

Marion Reporter (newspaper) clippings:
August 24, 1881: D.E. Crider and Mr. Freeman left for a protracted visit to Izzard County, Arkansas.

October 5, 1881: Davis Crider has returned from a visit to Arkansas.

July 26, 1882: Davis Crider to marry this evening to a popular young lady a few miles south of Marion.

♥ Davis married MARTHA ELLEN DEBOE July 26, 1882, in Crittenden Co., Kentucky, daughter of ABRAM DEBOE and MARY SMITH. She was born Mar. 22, 1861, in Crittenden Co., Kentucky, and died June 30, 1947, at Marion, Crittenden Co., Kentucky. Buried in Crayne Cemetery, Marion, Crittenden Co., Kentucky.

Children of DAVIS CRIDER and MARTHA DEBOE are:

91. i. NONA MAE6 CRIDER, b. April 18, 1883, Marion, Crittenden Co., Kentucky; d. October 4, 1966, Zillah, Yakima Co., Washington.

92.   ii. WILLIAM EWING CRIDER, b. July 31, 1884, Marion, Crittenden Co., Kentucky; d. January 6, 1967, Marion, Crittenden Co., Kentucky.

iii.   DENTON EUEL CRIDER, b. August 12, 1886, Marion, Crittenden Co., Kentucky. Buried: Crayne Cemetery, Marion, Crittenden Co., Kentucky

Denton never married.

iv. OTTIE SMITH CRIDER, b. January 28, 1888, Marion, Crittenden Co., Kentucky; d. Bef. 1900, Marion, Crittenden Co., Kentucky. Buried: Piney Fork Cem., Crittenden Co., Kentucky.

Reportedly Ottie, a male, died falling into a kettle of lye soap at an early age. He is buried near his grandfather, William, in Piney Fork Cemetery in an unmarked grave.

v. CARRIE ETTA CRIDER, b. November 3, 1888, Marion, Crittenden Co., Kentucky; d. Abt. 1922, Washington; m. RALPH T. NEWMAN, Crittenden Co., Kentucky.

Carrie and her husband had no children.

93.   vi. HOMER EVERETTE CRIDER, b. March 16, 1892, Marion, Crittenden Co., Kentucky; d. August 2, 1973, Marion, Crittenden Co., Kentucky.

94.   vii. EMMA LUELLA CRIDER, b. May 2, 1894, Marion, Crittenden Co., Kentucky; d. 1957, Marion, Crittenden Co., Kentucky.

viii. IDA VICTORIA CRIDER, b. July 3, 1896, Marion, Crittenden Co., Kentucky; d. May 23, 1969, Marion, Crittenden Co., Kentucky; buried: Crayne Cemetery, Marion, Crittenden Co., Kentucky; m. JOHN L. WRIGHT, Crittenden Co., Kentucky. Buried: Crayne Cemetery, Marion, Crittenden Co., Kentucky

ix. ALLIE JOE CRIDER, b. May 24, 1898, Marion, Crittenden Co., Kentucky; d. June 20, 1931, Marion, Crittenden Co., Kentucky. Buried: Crayne Cemetery, Marion, Crittenden Co., Kentucky.

Allie was reportedly shot and killed by a cousin, Hughey McCaslin.

95. x. WALLACE MCKINLEY CRIDER, b. October 23, 1900, Marion, Crittenden Co., Kentucky; d. February 1990, Marion, Crittenden Co., Kentucky.

64. FRANKLIN5 CRIDER *(THOMAS BENNETT4, DANIEL3, DANIEL2 KRIDER, JOHN MICHAEL1 KREIDER)* was born 1846 in Livingston Co., Kentucky.

♥ Franklin married MARIA MCCORMICK Bef. 1865 in Crittenden Co., Kentucky.

Child of FRANKLIN CRIDER and MARIA MCCORMICK is:

  i. LAURA ANN6 CRIDER, b. August 27, 1865, Marion, Crittenden Co., Kentucky; m. WILLIAM FLETCHER JACOBS, June 1, 1890, Marion, Crittenden Co., Kentucky.

65. LUCY JANE5 CRIDER *(DAVID4, JOHN3, DANIEL2 KRIDER, JOHN MICHAEL1 KREIDER)* was born December 19, 1840, in Pittsylvania Co., Virginia, and died in 1903 in Toshes, Pittsylvania Co., Virginia. Buried: Siloam Methodist, Toshes, Pittsylvania Co., Virginia

♥ Lucy married WINBORN R. TOSH April 11, 1861, in Pittsylvania Co., Virginia, son of GEORGE TOSH and LUCY, according to the marriage register. He was born Nov. 11, 1839, at Toshes, Pittsylvania

Co., Virginia, and died Oct. 18, 1891, at Toshes. Winborn is buried at Siloam Methodist, Toshes, Pittsylvania Co., Virginia.

Child of LUCY CRIDER and WINBORN TOSH is:

> i. JAMES A.6 TOSH, b. October 6, 1869, Pittsylvania Co., Virginia; d. June 26, 1886, Toshes, Pittsylvania Co., Virginia. Buried at Siloam Methodist, Toshes, Pittsylvania Co., Virginia.

66. GILLIE A.5 CRIDER *(DAVID4, JOHN3, DANIEL2 KRIDER, JOHN MICHAEL1 KREIDER)* was born March 12, 1848, in Pittsylvania Co., Virginia, and died October 23, 1922, in Toshes, Pittsylvania Co., Virginia. Buried at Siloam Methodist, Toshes, Pittsylvania Co., Virginia

♥ Gillie married REUBEN BENNETT March 26, 1871, in Pittsylvania Co., Virginia, son of JONATHAN BENNETT and MILDRED BAILEY. Reuben was born Dec. 3, 1848, in Pittsylvania Co., Virginia, and died Mar. 22, 1923, at Toshes, Pittsylvania Co., Virginia. He is buried at Siloam Methodist, Toshes, Pittsylvania Co., Virginia.

When Gillie married Reuben Bennett, her age was given as 23 years, and Reuben's was 22 years. Her parents were listed as David and Mary Crider. Reuben's parents were Jonathan and Mildred Bennett. The marriage was performed by Isiah Ramsey (husband of Matilda Bennett, widow of Henry Crider).

Children of GILLIE CRIDER and REUBEN BENNETT are:

> i. MARY E.6 BENNETT, b. July 1, 1872, Pittsylvania Co., Virginia; d. July 13, 1892, Toshes, Pittsylvania Co., Virginia.

Buried at Siloam Methodist, Toshes, Pittsylvania Co., Virginia.

    ii.   LAURA BELL BENNETT, b. October 21, 1880, Pittsylvania Co., Virginia; d. December 14, 1900, Toshes, Pittsylvania Co., Virginia. Buried at Siloam Methodist, Toshes, Pittsylvania Co., Virginia.

67. GEORGE DAVID5 CRIDER *(DAVID4, JOHN3, DANIEL2 KRIDER, JOHN MICHAEL1 KREIDER)* was born November 5, 1859, in Pittsylvania Co., Virginia, and died January 31, 1929, in Pittsylvania Co., Virginia. Buried: Sheva Church, Pittsylvania Co., Virginia

George married (1) SUSAN B. SHELHORSE January 2, 1879, in Pittsylvania Co., Virginia, daughter of JAMES SHELHORSE and SUSAN CRIDER. Susan was born in 1863 in Pittsylvania Co., Virginia, and died about 1887, also in Pittsylvania Co.

George was listed as 20 years old at his marriage to Susan. However, descendant Clyde B. East gives his birthdate as 3 November 1861. Susan was listed as 16 years old in the marriage register. Her parents were given as James M. and Susan (Crider) Shelhorse.

    Children of GEORGE CRIDER and SUSAN SHELHORSE are:

96.   i.   JAMES DANIEL6 CRIDER, b. October 3, 1879, Pittsylvania Co., Virginia; d. August 31, 1929, Toshes, Pittsylvania Co., Virginia.

97.   ii.   WILLIAM DAVID CRIDER, b. July 22, 1881, Toshes, Pittsylvania Co., Virginia; d. July 15, 1966, Pittsylvania Co., Virginia.

♥ George married (2) LUCY JACOBS Abt. 1889 in Pittsylvania Co., Virginia. Lucy was born about 1871 and died Jan. 29, 1927, at Meadows, Pittsylvania Co., Virginia.

Children of GEORGE CRIDER and LUCY JACOBS are:

iii. GEORGE ARON6 CRIDER, b. September 06, 1890, Toshes, Pittsylvania Co., Virginia; d. 1920, Sheva, Pittsylvania Co., Virginia.

George may have been mentally handicapped according to census records.

iv. JAMES R. CRIDER, b. December 23, 1891, Toshes, Pittsylvania Co., Virginia; d. 1919, Sheva, Pittsylvania Co., Virginia.

Jimmy was reportedly mentally handicapped.

98. v. MARY ELIZABETH CRIDER, b. December 20, 1892, Toshes, Pittsylvania Co., Virginia; d. December 6, 1937, Sheva, Pittsylvania Co., Virginia.

99. vi. JOHN HENRY CRIDER, b. February 13, 1894, Toshes, Pittsylvania Co., Virginia; d. July 20, 1955, Sheva, Pittsylvania Co., Virginia.

vii. DELIA BRANDON CRIDER, b. May 13, 1895, Toshes, Pittsylvania Co., Virginia; d. March 29, 1964, Sheva, Pittsylvania Co., Virginia; m. ABRAHAM RIDDLE, Pittsylvania Co., Virginia.

viii. EDWARD N. CRIDER, b. September 30, 1896, Toshes, Pittsylvania Co., Virginia; d. 1948, Sheva, Pittsylvania Co., Virginia.

Edward never married. He, like many of his siblings, was reportedly mentally handicapped.

ix. EFFIE PROSPERITY CRIDER, b. December 28, 1897, Toshes, Pittsylvania Co., Virginia; d. December 4, 1951, Sheva,

Pittsylvania Co., Virginia; m. OSCAR DAVIS, Pittsylvania Co., Virginia.

x. LUELLA CRIDER, b. April 30, 1900, Toshes, Pittsylvania Co., Virginia; d. April 24, 1962, Sheva, Pittsylvania Co., Virginia.

Luella never married.

xi. REUBEN BERKLEY CRIDER, b. February 22, 1901, Toshes, Pittsylvania Co., Virginia; d. April 15, 1983, Sheva, Pittsylvania Co., Virginia.

xii. CLAUDE PRICE CRIDER b. September 10, 1902, Meadows, Pittsylvania Co., Virginia; d. 1953, Sheva, Pittsylvania Co., Virginia.

Claude never married.

xiii. CLARENCE ALLEN CRIDER, b. March 22, 1904, Meadows, Pittsylvania Co., Virginia; d. April 23, 1973, Sheva, Pittsylvania Co., Virginia; m. CLARA BRUMFIELD, Pittsylvania Co., Virginia.

xiv. CARRIE MAYBELL CRIDER, b. September 2, 1905, Meadows, Pittsylvania Co., Virginia; d. August 26, 1976, Sheva, Pittsylvania Co., Virginia; m. RALEIGH ROBERTSON, Pittsylvania Co., Virginia.

xv. WYNDHAM REID CRIDER, b. 1907, Meadows, Pittsylvania Co., Virginia; d. 1931, Sheva, Pittsylvania Co., Virginia.

W. Reid was also reportedly mentally handicapped. He never married.

xvi. ERNEST HAIL CRIDER, b. April 16, 1909, Meadows, Pittsylvania Co., Virginia; d. January 14, 1964, Sheva, Pittsylvania Co., Virginia; m. HILDA F. FERREL, Pittsylvania Co., Virginia.

xvii. CHARLES GUY CRIDER, b. May 14, 1910, Meadows, Pittsylvania Co., Virginia; d. October 2, 1967, Sheva, Pittsylvania Co., Virginia; m. SALLIE MAY WELLS, August 18, 1942, Pittsylvania Co., Virginia.

xviii. OSCAR R. CRIDER, b. 1912, Meadows, Pittsylvania Co., Virginia; d. 1934, Sheva, Pittsylvania Co., Virginia.

Oscar was reportedly mentally handicapped. He never married.

xix. OTEY LEO CRIDER, b. October 23, 1913, Meadows, Pittsylvania Co., Virginia.

Otey never married.

xx. WALTER BARNARD CRIDER, b. June 8, 1915, Meadows, Pittsylvania Co., Virginia; d. January 11, 1974, Sheva, Pittsylvania Co., Virginia; m. MINNIE MABLE BROOKS, April 6, 1946, Pittsylvania Co., Virginia.

68. JAMES A.5 CRIDER *(DAVID4, GEORGE3, DANIEL2 KRIDER, JOHN MICHAEL1 KREIDER)* was born 1834 in Gibson Co., Tennessee, and died 1875 in Calloway Co., Kentucky.

James A. Crider was a farmer in Calloway County, listed in the 1860 census with no land but $660 in personal property. He was 26 years old, living with wife Elvira T., age 24, and daughter, A.J., age 4.

Family history states that James was a small boy when he followed his father, David, to feed the hogs. He was balancing himself on a rail fence when he fell and was attacked by a bobcat. David managed to scare off the bobcat, but not before James was badly mauled. David suspected the bobcat would return and went hunting with several neighbors. They found the bobcat sitting on a rock and shot him. Human flesh and hair embedded in the claws confirmed they had found the guilty party. James carried the scars of the encounter all his life, and when he was grown he wore a full beard to cover the scars (Robert E. Oliver, *The Ancestry of John Wesley Crider*, unpublished communication).

James Crider rode a mule to Tennessee on business one cold and rainy day. He returned home cold and wet and died of pneumonia the following morning (ibid.)

♥ James married ELVINA TENNESSEE THURMAN January 03, 1855, in Graves Co., Kentucky. She was born in 1836 at Maury Co., Tennessee.

In the marriage record of J.A. Crider and E.L. Thurmond, Elvina was said to be born in Maury County, Tennessee. She was 18 years old (Elvina's name is also given as Elvira in some records).

Elvina/Elvira was the daughter of James J. Thurman and Leah Hudspeth. James Thurman was born in 1808 in Virginia. Leah was born in 1810 in Maury County, Tennessee, the daughter of Thomas Hudspeth and Sarah Glen. Thomas was born in 1762 in Surrey County, North Carolina (Robert E. Oliver, unpublished communication).

Elvina was 24 years old in the 1860 census of Calloway County, Kentucky.

Children of JAMES CRIDER and ELVINA THURMAN are:

100.   i.   ANGELINE J.6 CRIDER, b. 1855, Calloway Co., Kentucky; d. 1922.
        ii.   ADA CRIDER, b. 1857, Calloway Co., Kentucky; m. IRA HAYES, November 4, 1886, Gibson Co., Tennessee.
        iii.   WILLIAM HUB CRIDER, b. 1858, Calloway Co., Kentucky; d. 1948; m. MYRTLE KILLEBREW.
        iv.   MARY CRIDER, b. August 4, 1859, Calloway Co., Kentucky.

            Mary reportedly died as a teenager (communication from Robert Oliver, Nixa, Missouri).

v. ROSA CRIDER, b. Abt. 1864, Calloway Co., Kentucky; m.
    JOHN R. NEWBILL, January 22, 1882, Gibson Co., Tennessee.
vi. JOHN WESLEY CRIDER, b. October 1872, Calloway Co.,
    Kentucky; d. January 1960, Campbell Co., Missouri; buried:
    Woodlawn Cem., Campbell Co., Missouri ; m. MAMIE
    LASSWELL.

John's father died when he was a young child. His mother
remarried a man named Melton and moved to Tennessee,
leaving her children with her oldest son, William, who "hired
them out." The 1880 census of Graves County shows John W.
Crider, age 8, living in the home of Ira Hayes, his uncle.

At the age of nineteen, John took his only possession, a mule,
and left for, Missouri. He stopped in Tennessee to collect his
mother, now widowed. She did not recognize him. John
secured a job at the Lasswell Lumber Company as a logger.
His size (over six feet tall) and strong body enabled him to
succeed in this physically demanding career. He was so
successful he rose to the position of Vice President.

John was a quiet man who didn't engage in small talk. Co-
workers said they could work beside him all day and he
wouldn't saw two words. His great-nephew, Clyde Oliver,
once said, "Uncle John didn't talk much, but when he did talk,
you'd better pay attention because he had something to say."

Years later, John told his children how he used to watch the
boss's daughter coming to the well each night to get water and
how beautiful she looked in her bonnet. After he found the
nerve to speak to Mamie Lasswell, they fell in love and
married. Mamie was the daughter of Joseph P. Lasswell and
Nancy Sirelda King. Joseph was the son of Daniel Lasswell
who moved to Missouri from North Carolina or Tennessee.
He owned a saw mill and a grist mill. One of his, employees
was William P. King, father of Nancy (her mother was Lavinia
Cox).

John owned 30,000 acres of Missouri farmland by the 1920's. This land was worked by many sharecroppers. As the decade ended, there were three straight years of floods, destroying crops. Also, the Depression began. When many tenants left town, taking horses and equipment, John declined to prosecute. However, he did suffer great financial losses, becoming bankrupt. He never regained his former wealth, but his farming did allow him to retire comfortably. (Robert E. Oliver, *The Ancestry of John Wesley Crider,* unpublished communication)

vii. STEVEN LINN CRIDER, b. 1874, Calloway Co., Kentucky.

69. LEE ANNA5 CRIDER *(DAVID4, GEORGE3, DANIEL2 KRIDER, JOHN MICHAEL1 KREIDER)* was born 1836 in Gibson Co., Tennessee. She was not married when her son James was born.

Child of LEE CRIDER:

i. JAMES E.6 CRIDER, b. 1857, Graves Co., Kentucky; d. 1930, Kentucky; m. MARY ELIZABETH WAGGONER, Kentucky.

James' death certificate confirms he was illegitimate. He was living in the home of his grandparents, David and Sarah, in the 1860 census of Graves County, Kentucky, along with Lee Anna Crider, age 24. His death certificate gives his mother as Paralee Miller. Lee Anna Crider married Benjamin Miller before 1870 when they appeared in the census living next door to David and Sarah Crider.

70. RACHEL R.5 CRIDER *(DAVID4, GEORGE3, DANIEL2 KRIDER, JOHN MICHAEL1 KREIDER)* was born October 10, 1840, in Calloway Co., Kentucky.

♥ Rachel married GEORGE T. HANELINE October 26, 1858, in Graves Co., Kentucky. George was born Dec. 4, 1838, in Kentucky.

In the 1860 census of Calloway County, Kentucky, George Haneline and wife Rachel owned $350 in land and $485 in personal property. They had no children listed. They were living three farms from Elijah Haneline, age 64, probable father of George. Elijah's wife was listed as Elizabeth, age 56. Both were born in North Carolina. In the home of Elijah and Elizabeth were Hope H., male, age 16, and Sarah E., age 12, both born in Kentucky. Elijah was a farmer with $2600 in land and $4936 in personal property. Next door to them in the opposite direction, was Daniel Haneline, age 39, farmer, with $1400 in land and $1003 in property. Daniel's wife was Amanda J., age 29. Both were born in Tennessee. Their children, all born in Kentucky, were John, age 16, Elijah, age 14, and William D., age 12. Also living in their home was Wesley B. Hicks, age 22, who owned $302 in personal property.

George and Rachel's birth dates and marriage date, along with the birthdates of their children, were found in the Haneline family Bible, owned by Mrs. Walter W. Johnson of Paducah, Kentucky (LDS Microfilm #301102).

Children of RACHEL CRIDER and GEORGE HANELINE are:

     i.   ORKNEY E.6 HANELINE, b. November 7, 1859, Kentucky.
    ii.   BETTIE HANELINE, b. September 23, 1861, Kentucky; d. March 16, 1927, Kentucky.

71. ROBERT WALKER5 CRIDER *(DAVID4, GEORGE3, DANIEL2 KRIDER, JOHN MICHAEL1 KREIDER)* was born 1848 in Calloway Co., Kentucky, and died October, 1880, in Pocahontas, Randolph Co., Arkansas.

Robert's death date was found in the Bible owned by John W. Crider of Graves Co. Kentucky (LDS Microfilm #301102).

♥ Robert married MARGARET ISABELLA KIDD October 11, 1869, in Graves Co., Kentucky. She died in 1921 in Mayfield, Graves Co., Kentucky.

Children of ROBERT CRIDER and MARGARET KIDD are:

- i. CORA ELLEN6 CRIDER, b. 1871, Graves Co., Kentucky.
- ii. JAMES L. CRIDER, b. 1874, Graves Co., Kentucky.
- iii. THOMAS C. CRIDER, b. 1875, Graves Co., Kentucky.
- iv. JOHN WALKER CRIDER, b. 1877, Pocahontas, Randolph Co., Arkansas; d. Aft. 1961.

72. JAMES WINSLOW5 CRIDER *(THOMAS BENNETT4, GEORGE3, DANIEL2 KRIDER, JOHN MICHAEL1 KREIDER)* was born September 25, 1851, in Gibson Co., Tennessee, and died December 18, 1924, in Bradford, Gibson Co., Tennessee. Buried: December 1924, Antioch Cemetery, Bradford, Gibson Co., Tennessee

James W. Crider was a pharmacist. He received his education in McKenzie, Carroll County, Tennessee. He died of yellow fever, leaving his only surviving Anita, with a large inheritance.

♥ James married ANNA REECE REED Bef. 1889 in Gibson Co., Tennessee, daughter of H. WASHINGTON REED and ELIZABETH ARNOLD. Anna was born Aug. 29, 1862, in Wilson Co., Tennessee, and died Dec. 21, 1937, at Corinth, Alcorn Co., Mississippi.

Anna Reed was a teacher in a one-room schoolhouse when she met James Crider. She received her education at Bethel College in Tennessee.

She died while living with her daughter, Anita, in Corinth. She was buried at Antioch Cemetery, Bradford, Gibson Co., Tennessee

Children of JAMES CRIDER and ANNA REED are:

     i.   HALLIE6 CRIDER, b. August 04, 1889, Bradford, Gibson Co., Tennessee; d. August 31, 1892, Bradford, Gibson Co., Tennessee. Buried: September 1892, Antioch Cemetery, Gibson Co., Tennessee

     ii.   RUTH CRIDER, b. Abt. 1891, Bradford, Gibson Co., Tennessee; d. Bradford, Gibson Co., Tennessee.

            Ruth Crider died the day she was born. Her birthdate is unknown at this time.

101.   iii.   EMMOGENE ANITA CRIDER, b. March 05, 1902, Bradford, Gibson Co., Tennessee; d. July 19, 1992, Corinth, Alcorn Co., Mississippi.

73. PRESTON COLUMBUS5 CRIDER *(DANIEL BENNETT4, GEORGE3, DANIEL2 KRIDER, JOHN MICHAEL1 KREIDER)* was born November 1843, in Bradford, Gibson Co., Tennessee, and died in February, 1918, in Bradford, Gibson Co., Tennessee.

♥ Preston married SARAH VICTORIA DOWLAND December 16, 1870, in Gibson Co., Tennessee. Sarah was born Feb. 9, 1854, at Bradford, Gibson Co., Tennessee. She died July 30, 1922 at Bradford and is buried at Shiloh Baptist Cemetery, Gibson, Tennessee.

Children of PRESTON CRIDER and SARAH DOWLAND are:

102.   i.   LONZO WELDON6 CRIDER, b. October 8, 1871, Gibson Co., Tennessee; d. March 12, 1940, Gibson Co., Tennessee.

103.   ii.   ADA FLORENCE CRIDER, b. August 23, 1873, Bradford, Gibson Co., Tennessee; d. March 1, 1962, Milan, Gibson Co., Tennessee.

        iii.   H. NEELY CRIDER, b. February 3, 1876, Skullbone, Gibson Co., Tennessee; d. 1955, Gibson Co., Tennessee. Buried: Shiloh Bapt. Cem., Gibson Co., Tennessee

        iv.   CHARLES CRIDER, b. February 18, 1879, Bradford, Gibson Co., Tennessee; m. COLLIE SELLERS.

        v.   TIMOTHY CRIDER, b. February 18, 1879, Bradford, Gibson Co., Tennessee; m. ILIE.

        vi.   WILLIAM EDWARD CRIDER, b. August 25, 1884, Bradford, Gibson Co., Tennessee; d. February 25, 1950, Gibson Co., Tennessee; m. VERA GREEN JOHNS.

        vii.   JACK HALL CRIDER, b. October 22, 1886, Bradford, Gibson Co., Tennessee; d. Gibson Co., Tennessee; buried: Bradford Cem., Gibson Co., Tennessee; m. ELLA OSTEEN.

        viii.   SALLIE CRIDER, b. Abt. 1889, Skullbone, Gibson Co., Tennessee.

        ix.   AGGIE CRIDER, b. Abt. 1890, Skullbone, Gibson Co., Tennessee.

        x.   WEAVER P. CRIDER, b. 1892, Bradford, Gibson Co., Tennessee; d. Gibson Co., Tennessee; m. LAURA "LURA" M. AIKEN, Gibson Co., Tennessee. They were both buried at Locust Grove Cemetery, Gibson Co., Tennessee.

74. MILTON E.5 CRIDER *(GEORGE W.4, GEORGE3, DANIEL2 KRIDER, JOHN MICHAEL1 KREIDER)* was born December 19, 1842, in Calloway Co., Kentucky.

♥   Milton married JANE WEST in Kentucky.

Child of MILTON CRIDER and JANE WEST is:

104.   i.   JOHN WESLEY6 CRIDER, b. July 8, 1869, Calloway Co.,
              Kentucky.

75. FELIX HENRY5 CRIDER *(RICHARD HENRY4, HENRY3, DANIEL2
KRIDER, JOHN MICHAEL1 KREIDER)* was born October 19, 1838, in
Carroll Co., Tennessee, and died September 19, 1924, in Carroll Co.,
Tennessee.

♥ Felix married LARCENIA ELIZABETH LAYCOOK in 1861 in
Tennessee, daughter of JOSEPH LAYCOOK and ANNIE SUGGS. She was
born May 7, 1845, at Carroll Co., Tennessee, and died in January,
1925, also at Carroll Co., Tennessee.

Felix and Larcenia were farmers in the Palmer Shelter community of
Carroll County.

Children of FELIX CRIDER and LARCENIA LAYCOOK are:

        i.   EDIE A.6 CRIDER, b. March 10, 1862, Carroll Co., Tennessee;
             d. November 21, 1921; m. JOHN HILL, February 25, 1882,
             Carroll Co., Tennessee.
       ii.   FRANCES ISABELLA CRIDER, b. August 18, 1864, Carroll Co.,
             Tennessee; d. July 1, 1942; m. LEWIS VICKERS, November 16,
             1896, Carroll Co., Tennessee.
      iii.   RICHARD SAMUEL CRIDER, b. November 24, 1868, Carroll
             Co., Tennessee; d. December 23, 1934; m. MARTHA KING,
             November 5, 1891, Carroll Co., Tennessee.
       iv.   EXIE LOUISE CRIDER, b. June 28, 1870, Carroll Co.,
             Tennessee; d. November 3, 1935.
105.   v.   RICHARD ALBERT CRIDER, b. July 2, 1877, Palmer Shelter,
             Carroll Co., Tennessee; d. October 23, 1952, Carroll Co.,
             Tennessee.

	vi.	MARY ETTA CRIDER, b. June 24, 1879, Carroll Co., Tennessee; d. May 24, 1972; m. JOHN W. DILL.
106.	vii.	JOSIE NEVADA CRIDER, b. August 10, 1881, Carroll Co., Tennessee; d. May 6, 1966, Perry Co., Tennessee.
	viii.	DORA ADA CRIDER, b. September 10, 1881, Carroll Co., Tennessee; d. January 25, 1981; m. W. H. WILKES.
	ix.	PERMELIA ELIZABETH CRIDER, b. September 19, 1884, Carroll Co., Tennessee; d. December 28, 1956; m. JESSE OATSVALL.

76. ALLEN5 HOLLADAY *(CATHERINE4 CRIDER, HENRY3, DANIEL2 KRIDER, JOHN MICHAEL1 KREIDER)* was born December 5, 1851, in Carroll Co., Tennessee, and died August 2, 1928, in Carroll Co., Tennessee.

♥ Allen married SARAH BATHSHEBA UTLEY April 28, 1880, in Benton Co., Tennessee. Sarah was born about 1855 at Benton Co., Tennessee.

Child of ALLEN HOLLADAY and SARAH UTLEY is:

107.	i.	CARLIE B.6 HOLLADAY, b. September 30, 1882, Benton Co., Tennessee; d. January 24, 1965, Perry Co., Tennessee.

77. ROBERT MONROE5 CRIDER *(JAMES CARROLL4, HENRY3, DANIEL2 KRIDER, JOHN MICHAEL1 KREIDER)* was born 1868 in Carroll Co., Tennessee, and died January 27, 1931, in Carroll Co., Tennessee.

♥ Robert married MARTHA A. ROSS January 5, 1892, in Tennessee. Martha is buried at Hampton Cemetery, Carroll Co., Tennessee

Children of ROBERT CRIDER and MARTHA ROSS are:

    i.   GAITHER6 CRIDER, b. Abt. 1894, Tennessee; m. DON HAMPTON.
    ii.   THOMAS B. CRIDER, b. Abt. 1896, Tennessee.
    iii. ELLIE G. CRIDER, b. Abt. 1900, Tennessee.
108.   iv. HOMER LEE CRIDER, b. 1903, Carroll Co., Tennessee; d. 1960, Carroll Co., Tennessee.

78. ARAMINTA5 CRIDER *(DANIEL W.4, SAMUEL3, DANIEL2 KRIDER, JOHN MICHAEL1 KREIDER)* was born August 22, 1833, in Kentucky, and died January 16, 1852, in Kentucky.

♥ Araminta married her cousin, WILLIAM BENNETT CRIDER September 3, 1849, in Livingston Co., Kentucky, son of HENRY CRIDER and CATHERINE CRIDER (see earlier entry for William Bennett Crider).

Araminta died in childbirth. Her son was born dead.
    Child of ARAMINTA CRIDER and WILLIAM CRIDER is:

    i.   BABY BOY6 CRIDER, b. January 15, 1852, Livingston Co., Kentucky; d. January 15, 1852, Livingston Co., Kentucky.

       This child was still-born.

79. SUSAN B.5 SHELHORSE *(SUSAN C.4 CRIDER, WILLIAM B.3, DANIEL2 KRIDER, JOHN MICHAEL1 KREIDER)* was born in 1863 in Pittsylvania Co., Virginia, and died Abt. 1887 in Pittsylvania Co., Virginia.

♥ Susan married her cousin, GEORGE DAVID CRIDER, January 2, 1879, in Pittsylvania Co., Virginia, son of DAVID CRIDER and MARY EDWARDS.

Susan was listed as 16 years old in the marriage register. Her parents were given as James M. and Susan (Crider) Shelhorse. George was listed as 20 years old at his marriage to Susan. However, descendant, Clyde B. East gives his birthdate as November 3, 1861.

Children of SUSAN SHELHORSE and GEORGE CRIDER are:

96.   i.   JAMES DANIEL6 CRIDER, b. October 3, 1879, Pittsylvania Co., Virginia; d. August 31, 1929, Toshes, Pittsylvania Co., Virginia.

97.   ii.   WILLIAM DAVID CRIDER, b. July 22, 1881, Toshes, Pittsylvania Co., Virginia; d. July 15, 1966, Pittsylvania Co., Virginia.

SIXTH GENERATION

80. ALLEN TOM6 CRIDER *(JOHN HENRY5, HENRY4, DANIEL3, DANIEL2 KRIDER, JOHN MICHAEL1 KREIDER)* was born November 30, 1839, in Livingston Co., Kentucky, and died November 24, 1866.

♥ Allen married ELLEN JANE MCDOWELL Bef. 1863 in Kentucky.

Child of ALLEN CRIDER and ELLEN MCDOWELL is:

109. i. FRANCIS NEWTON7 CRIDER, b. February 25, 1863, Crittenden Co., Kentucky; d. January 11, 1942, Mesa Co., Colorado.

81. JASPER GROOMS6 CRIDER *(JOHN HENRY5, HENRY4, DANIEL3, DANIEL2 KRIDER, JOHN MICHAEL1 KREIDER)* was born August 23, 1841 in Livingston Co., Kentucky, and died September 25, 1908

♥ Jasper married LYDIA LOWRY Bef. 1871 in Kentucky.

Child of JASPER CRIDER and LYDIA LOWRY is:

  i. LURENA FLORENCE7 CRIDER, b. February 2, 1871, Caldwell Co., Kentucky; m. HENRY NEWTON CANNON, August 9, 1888, Princeton, Caldwell Co., Kentucky.

82. WILLIAM H.6 CRIDER *(JOHN HENRY5, HENRY4, DANIEL3, DANIEL2 KRIDER, JOHN MICHAEL1 KREIDER)* was born November 29, 1851 in

Crittenden Co., Kentucky, and died January 7, 1935 in Phillips Co., Kansas.

♥ William married MARY LOUISE CANNON March 8, 1874 in Princeton, Caldwell Co., Kentucky, daughter of JOHN CANNON and LAMIRA FOSTER.

William and Mary were married at the home of John C. Fralick (her mother's home). Jacob L. Hughey, cousin of the groom, performed the rites. The witnesses were J.C. James and Finis S. Lowery.

They were tobacco farmers in Fredonia, Kentucky, until their move to Kansas in 1885. They traveled by train with their four small sons, aged four to ten, to Kirwin, Kansas which was the end of the railroad at that time. They traveled on another 20 miles to Phillipsburg, Kansas. Mary's brothers, Finish and F.B. Cannon, had settled there previously and helped William secure a patent of 160 acres adjoining F.B.'s property (Ruth Crider Drake, *Caldwell County Heritage Book*).

   Children of WILLIAM CRIDER and MARY CANNON are:

      i.   EDDIE ORRIN7 CRIDER, b. February 5, 1875, Princeton, Caldwell Co., Kentucky; d. 1927.

          E. Orrin was elected to County Clerk's office of Phillips County, Kansas, in 1926.

110.   ii. GEORGE VERNON CRIDER, b. May 6, 1877, Princeton, Caldwell Co., Kentucky; d. 1956.

     iii. FELIX LOGAN CRIDER, b. November 2, 1879, Princeton, Caldwell Co., Kentucky; d. 1956.

     iv. WILLIAM EVIN CRIDER, b. April 8, 1881, Princeton, Caldwell Co., Kentucky; d. 1950.

William E. served in the Kansas legislature from 1937 to 1940.

    v.   LEWRANEY J. CRIDER, b. 1887, Phillipsburg, Phillips Co., Kansas; d. 1971.

   vi. SARAH A. CRIDER, b. 1890, Phillipsburg, Phillips Co., Kansas; d. 1918.

83. ZACHARIAH JOHNSON6 CRIDER *(JACOB EWING5, JACOB B.4, JACOB3, DANIEL2 KRIDER, JOHN MICHAEL1 KREIDER)* was born in 1871 in Caldwell Co., Kentucky, and died 1932 in Caldwell Co., Kentucky. Buried in 1932, Fredonia Cem., Caldwell Co., Kentucky.

Zachariah, Jr., obtained a law degree in New York State and practiced law in Marion, Kentucky. He also managed his father's large farm in Fredonia.

♥ Zachariah married ANNA CECELIA ROCHE 1907 in Kentucky. Buried in Fredonia Cem., Caldwell Co., Kentucky.

Children of ZACHARIAH CRIDER and ANNA ROCHE are:

111.   i.   EMMETT COOPER7 CRIDER, b. 1908, Caldwell Co., Kentucky; d. 1967.

112.   ii. ZACHARIAH JOHNSON CRIDER III, b. 1911, Caldwell Co., Kentucky; d. 1972.

113.   iii. ALICE CRIDER, b. 1914, Caldwell Co., Kentucky.

114.   iv. NELL CRIDER, b. 1914, Caldwell Co., Kentucky.

        v.   JACOB EWING CRIDER III, b. 1916, Caldwell Co., Kentucky; d. 1944 in England.

Jacob died fighting in WWII. He was a co-pilot and died in a plane crash. He was awarded the Purple Heart posthumously

(Cynthia Kay Crider Whitsett, *Caldwell County Heritage Book*).

    vi. JOSEPH KEENE CRIDER, b. 1918, Caldwell Co., Kentucky; d. 1986.

   vii. FORREST WAYNE CRIDER, b. 1920, Caldwell Co., Kentucky; d. 1942, Java Sea.

Forrest, like his brother Jacob, died fighting in WWII. His naval ship sank in the Java Sea. He was awarded the Purple Heart posthumously. Buried in 1942, Fredonia Cem., Caldwell Co., Kentucky

115.   viii. JANE CRIDER, b. 1922, Caldwell Co., Kentucky; d. 1980.

84. JACOB EWING6 CRIDER , JR. *(JACOB EWING5, JACOB B.4, JACOB3, DANIEL2 KRIDER, JOHN MICHAEL1 KREIDER)* was born 1880 in Caldwell Co., Kentucky, and died 1950 in Caldwell Co., Kentucky. Buried: Fredonia Cem., Caldwell Co., Kentucky

Jacob, Jr., worked with his father and brother on the family farm.

♥ Jacob married ISABEL HOWERTON in 1913 in Caldwell Co., Kentucky.

Child of JACOB CRIDER and ISABEL HOWERTON is:

    i. WYCKLIFFE WYATT7 CRIDER.

85. MARY MELISSA6 CRIDER *(WILLIAM BRADLEY5, WILLIAM M.4, JACOB3, DANIEL2 KRIDER, JOHN MICHAEL1 KREIDER)* was born September 23, 1859 in Cochran Hill, Crittenden Co., Kentucky, and died in 1938 in Marion, Crittenden Co., Kentucky. Buried in Chapel Hill Cem., Marion, Crittenden Co., Kentucky

♥ Mary married HENRY O. HILL January 5, 1881 in Crittenden Co., Kentucky.

Children of MARY CRIDER and HENRY HILL are:

    i.   EARL7 HILL, b. Abt. 1883, Marion, Crittenden Co., Kentucky.
    ii. GRACE HILL, b. Abt. 1885, Marion, Crittenden Co., Kentucky.
    iii. RUTH HILL, b. Abt. 1887, Marion, Crittenden Co., Kentucky.
    iv. ELVA HILL, b. Abt. 1889, Marion, Crittenden Co., Kentucky.
    v.   ADA HILL, b. Abt. 1891, Marion, Crittenden Co., Kentucky.

86. GEORGE HARRIS6 CRIDER *(WILLIAM BRADLEY5, WILLIAM M.4, JACOB3, DANIEL2 KRIDER, JOHN MICHAEL1 KREIDER)* was born March 7, 1862 in Marion, Crittenden Co., Kentucky.

According to the Marion Reporter (newspaper), George traveled to Missouri to find a new home for his father and family in February 1881. He returned two weeks later, "satisfied Kentucky will make a better home."

♥ George married FULTON HAYNES in Kentucky.

Children of GEORGE CRIDER and FULTON HAYNES are:

    i.   HOMER C.7 CRIDER, b. Marion, Crittenden Co., Kentucky.
    ii. RUTH CRIDER, b. Marion, Crittenden Co., Kentucky.
    iii. MARY CRIDER, b. Marion, Crittenden Co., Kentucky.
    iv. MARGUERITE CRIDER, b. Marion, Crittenden Co., Kentucky.

87. MILTON BIRD6 CRIDER *(WILLIAM BRADLEY5, WILLIAM M.4, JACOB3, DANIEL2 KRIDER, JOHN MICHAEL1 KREIDER)* was born July 9, 1870, in Marion, Crittenden Co., Kentucky, and died March 19, 1920, in Marshall, Saline Co., Missouri. Buried at Mt. Olive Cem., Marshall, Saline Co., Missouri

♥ Milton married MAE ALMA BALLENTINE in Kentucky. Alma was born Jan. 7, 1876 in Marshall, Saline Co., Missouri, and died on June 21, 1962 in Marshall, Saline Co., Missouri. She was buried at Ridge Park Cem., Marshall, Saline Co., Missouri

Children of MILTON CRIDER and MAE BALLENTINE are:

      i. MARTHA LUCILLE7 CRIDER, b. July 23, 1900, Marshall, Saline Co., Missouri; d. September 16, 1961, Marshall, Saline Co., Missouri.

          Martha never married.

116.   ii. DAISY FRANCES CRIDER, b. October 19, 1903, Marshall, Saline Co., Missouri.

117.   iii. MILTON R. CRIDER, b. September 29, 1905, Marshall, Saline Co., Missouri.

      iv. KATHRYN MAE CRIDER, b. June 12, 1908, Marshall, Saline Co., Missouri.

118.   v. JOSEPH BALLENTINE CRIDER, b. December 19, 1911, Marshall, Saline Co., Missouri; d. August 28, 1967, Jonesboro, Craighead Co., Arkansas.

88. ALBERT FOSTER6 CRIDER *(WILLIAM BRADLEY5, WILLIAM M.4, JACOB3, DANIEL2 KRIDER, JOHN MICHAEL1 KREIDER)* was born

January 13, 1873, in Marion, Crittenden Co., Kentucky, and died September 9, 1945, in Shreveport, Caddo Co., Louisiana.

♥ Albert married ROSA RHEE KEVIL in Kentucky, daughter of G. BELL KEVIL.

Children of ALBERT CRIDER and ROSA KEVIL are:

119. i. FOSTER KEVIL7 CRIDER, b. March 3, 1907.
120. ii. NOEL MONTGOMERY CRIDER, b. December 25, 1908.

89. LAWRENCE EDWIN6 CRIDER *(WILLIAM BRADLEY5, WILLIAM M.4, JACOB3, DANIEL2 KRIDER, JOHN MICHAEL1 KREIDER)* was born July 10, 1875, in Marion, Crittenden Co., Kentucky, and died August 6, 1942, in Marion, Crittenden Co., Kentucky. Buried at Marion Cem., Crittenden Co., Kentucky.

♥ Lawrence married MAUD HILL in Crittenden Co., Kentucky. Maude was born Dec. 10, 1878, in Crayne, Crittenden Co., Kentucky, and died Nov. 11, 1972, in Marion, Crittenden Co., Kentucky. Buried at Mapleview Cem., Marion, Crittenden Co., Kentucky.

Children of LAWRENCE CRIDER and MAUD HILL are:

121. i. HUBERT DIXON7 CRIDER, b. January 21, 1903, Marion, Crittenden Co., Kentucky.
122. ii. MARTHA VIRGINIA CRIDER, b. April 3, 1911, Marion, Crittenden Co., Kentucky.

90. JACOB HUGHEY6 CRIDER *(WILLIAM BRADLEY5, WILLIAM M.4, JACOB3, DANIEL2 KRIDER, JOHN MICHAEL1 KREIDER)* was born December 19, 1877, in Marion, Crittenden Co., Kentucky, and died April 3, 1952, in Marion, Crittenden Co., Kentucky.

♥ Jacob married ADA WATSON March 24, 1909, in Crittenden Co., Kentucky. Ada was born June 29, 1883, at New Salem, Crittenden Co., Kentucky.

Children of JACOB CRIDER and ADA WATSON are:

123.	i.	ALBERT THOMPSON7 CRIDER, b. December 22, 1909, Marion, Crittenden Co., Kentucky.
124.	ii.	WILLIAM EDWIN CRIDER, b. December 12, 1917, Marion, Crittenden Co., Kentucky.
125.	iii.	SARAH JANETTE CRIDER, b. September 05, 1921, Crittenden Co., Kentucky.

91. NONA MAE6 CRIDER *(DAVIS EWING5, WILLIAM M.4, JACOB3, DANIEL2 KRIDER, JOHN MICHAEL1 KREIDER)* was born April 18, 1883 in Marion, Crittenden Co., Kentucky, and died October 4, 1966 in Zillah, Yakima Co., Washington.

♥ Nona married GEORGE PETER STOVALL Bef. 1905 in Crittenden Co., Kentucky. George was born July 29, 1882 in Crittenden Co., Kentucky, and died on March 30, 1951 in Zillah, Yakima Co., Washington.

Nona and her family moved to Washington State in 1905, along with many other Crittenden County families.

Children of NONA CRIDER and GEORGE STOVALL are:

    i.   WILLIAM EDWARD7 STOVALL.
   ii.   VERA STOVALL.
  iii.   VELDA STOVALL.
  iv.   ELDON STOVALL.

92. WILLIAM EWING6 CRIDER *(DAVIS EWING5, WILLIAM M.4, JACOB3, DANIEL2 KRIDER, JOHN MICHAEL1 KREIDER)* was born July 31, 1884, in Marion, Crittenden Co., Kentucky, and died January 6, 1967, in Marion, Crittenden Co., Kentucky. Buried: Crayne Cemetery, Marion, Crittenden Co., Kentucky.

♥ William married ROSE FOWLER THOMPSON in Crittenden Co., Kentucky. Rose was born September 26, 1898, at Crittenden Co., Kentucky and died March 15, 1968, at Marion, Crittenden Co., Kentucky. Buried at Crayne Cemetery, Marion, Crittenden Co., Kentucky.

Children of WILLIAM CRIDER and ROSE THOMPSON are:

     i.   JUANITA7 CRIDER, b. 1920, Crittenden Co., Kentucky.
    ii.   MARTHA CRIDER, b. Abt. 1922, Crittenden Co., Kentucky.
   iii.   WILLIAM EWING CRIDER , JR., b. 1924, Crittenden Co., Kentucky; d. 1957.
   iv.   ROBERT EWING CRIDER, b. August 08, 1926, Crittenden Co., Kentucky; d. August 12, 1985, Marion, Crittenden Co., Kentucky; m. BILLIE DORIS COWAN, June 4, 1966, Crittenden Co., Kentucky.
    v.   ROSA NELL CRIDER, b. Abt. 1928, Crittenden Co., Kentucky.
   vi.   JAMES C. CRIDER, b. Abt. 1930, Crittenden Co., Kentucky.
  vii.   CLAUDINE CRIDER, b. Abt. 1932, Crittenden Co., Kentucky.
 viii.   LONNIE CRIDER, b. Abt. 1933, Crittenden Co., Kentucky; m. ARDELL CRAZE, Fort Payne, DeKalb Co., Alabama.
   ix.   WAYNE CRIDER, b. Abt. 1934, Crittenden Co., Kentucky.

x. HELEN CRIDER, b. Abt. 1935.
xi. PHYLLIS CRIDER, b. Abt. 1936, Crittenden Co., Kentucky.
xii. MADELINE CRIDER, b. Abt. 1938, Crittenden Co., Kentucky.

93. HOMER EVERETTE6 CRIDER *(DAVIS EWING5, WILLIAM M.4, JACOB3, DANIEL2 KRIDER, JOHN MICHAEL1 KREIDER)* was born March 16, 1892, in Marion, Crittenden Co., Kentucky, and died August 2, 1973, in Marion, Crittenden Co., Kentucky. Buried at Crayne Cemetery, Crittenden Co., Kentucky.

♥ Homer married REABEATH CAMPBELL in Crittenden Co., Kentucky. She was buried at Crayne Cemetery, Crittenden Co., Kentucky.

Children of HOMER CRIDER and REABEATH CAMPBELL are:

| | i. | LULA IRENE7 CRIDER, b. Crittenden Co., Kentucky. |
| 126. | ii. | NORMAN J. CRIDER, b. March 16, 1892, Crittenden Co., Kentucky; d. August 4, 1973, Crittenden Co., Kentucky. |

94. EMMA LUELLA6 CRIDER *(DAVIS EWING5, WILLIAM M.4, JACOB3, DANIEL2 KRIDER, JOHN MICHAEL1 KREIDER)* was born May 2, 1894, in Marion, Crittenden Co., Kentucky, and died in 1957 in Marion, Crittenden Co., Kentucky. Buried at Crayne Cemetery, Marion, Crittenden Co., Kentucky.

♥ Emma married HOMER HUGHES in Crittenden Co., Kentucky.

Children of EMMA CRIDER and HOMER HUGHES are:

i. BRUCE7 HUGHES, b. Crittenden Co., Kentucky.
ii. MILDRED HUGHES, b. Crittenden Co., Kentucky.

95. WALLACE MCKINLEY6 CRIDER *(DAVIS EWING5, WILLIAM M.4, JACOB3, DANIEL2 KRIDER, JOHN MICHAEL1 KREIDER)* was born October 23, 1900, in Marion, Crittenden Co., Kentucky, and died in February 1990, in Marion, Crittenden Co., Kentucky. Buried at Crayne Cemetery, Marion, Crittenden Co., Kentucky.

♥ Wallace married EDNA MAY RYAN August 12, 1934, in Crittenden Co., Kentucky. Edna was born August 24, 1911, in Crittenden Co., Kentucky.

Children of WALLACE CRIDER and EDNA RYAN are:

127.   i. WALLACE7 CRIDER, b. October 29, 1935, Mott City, Crittenden Co., Kentucky; d. April 4, 1987, Crittenden Co., Kentucky.
      ii. CHARLES GLENN CRIDER, b. February 26, 1943, Mott City, Crittenden Co., Kentucky.

Charles and his family live in Union County, Kentucky.

96. JAMES DANIEL6 CRIDER *(GEORGE DAVID5, DAVID4, JOHN3, DANIEL2 KRIDER, JOHN MICHAEL1 KREIDER)* was born October 03, 1879, in Pittsylvania Co., Virginia, and died August 31, 1929 in Toshes, Pittsylvania Co., Virginia. Buried at Siloam Methodist, Toshes, Pittsylvania Co., Virginia.

James Daniel's birth and death dates were taken from his tombstone at Siloam Methodist Church. He was born in the Toshes area and lived there most of his life. Daniel was a farmer, sawmill operator and storekeeper at different periods of his life. He married Lenore about 1915-16. She died a few months after the birth of their first child, Leo, who was raised by his maternal grandmother. Daniel married again about 1927-28 to Anna Edwards who was born in Toshes but whose family had moved to Mississippi when she was a child. She was 10-15 years younger than Daniel. There were no children from this marriage, and Anna returned to Mississippi after Daniel's death.

♥ James married LENORE CREASEY in Pittsylvania Co., Virginia.

Child of JAMES CRIDER and LENORE CREASEY is:

    i.   LEO7 CRIDER, b. December 19, 1918, Pittsylvania Co., Virginia; m. BERTHA SHIELDS, April 19, 1947.

        Leo was raised by his grandmother Creasey after his mother's death when he was two or three months old. He served in WWII in the 1st Armored Division and received a serious wound at the Anzio Beachhead in 1944. He was discharged from the military in 1944 with a full disability. He married Bertha in 1947; they have no children. He worked over 30 years with the Virginia Highway Department. He and Bertha are retired and living in Gretna, Virginia (1992).

97. WILLIAM DAVID6 CRIDER *(GEORGE DAVID5, DAVID4, JOHN3, DANIEL2 KRIDER, JOHN MICHAEL1 KREIDER)* was born July 22, 1881, in Toshes, Pittsylvania Co., Virginia, and died July 15, 1966, in Pittsylvania Co., Virginia.

Will's mother, Susan, died when he was a young child.

♥ William married OLIVE HUGHEY. She was born July 18, 1891 in Pittsylvania Co., Virginia, and died June 11, 1979.

Children of WILLIAM CRIDER and OLIVE HUGHEY are:

    i.   HUGHEY L.7 CRIDER, b. July 13, 1917, Pittsylvania Co., Virginia; d. September 18, 1987, Pittsylvania Co., Virginia. Buried: Gretna Bur. Park, Gretna, Pittsylvania Co., Virginia

    ii.   ROSCOE CARLOS CRIDER, b. February 9, 1920, Pittsylvania Co., Virginia; d. April 13, 1977.

    iii.   PORTIA CRIDER, b. March 25, 1923, Pittsylvania Co., Virginia.

    iv.   JEAN CRIDER, b. April 26, 1937, Pittsylvania Co., Virginia.

98. MARY ELIZABETH6 CRIDER *(GEORGE DAVID5, DAVID4, JOHN3, DANIEL2 KRIDER, JOHN MICHAEL1 KREIDER)* was born December 20, 1892, in Toshes, Pittsylvania Co., Virginia, and died December 6, 1937, in Sheva, Pittsylvania Co., Virginia.

♥ Mary married JAMES SMITH EAST January 28, 1912 in Pittsylvania Co., Virginia.

Child of MARY CRIDER and JAMES EAST is:

128.   i.   CLYDE BENNETT7 EAST, b. July 19, 1921, Coles Hill, Pittsylvania Co., Virginia.

99. JOHN HENRY6 CRIDER *(GEORGE DAVID5, DAVID4, JOHN3, DANIEL2 KRIDER, JOHN MICHAEL1 KREIDER)* was born February 13, 1894, in Toshes, Pittsylvania Co., Virginia, and died July 20, 1955, in Sheva, Pittsylvania Co., Virginia.

♥ John married MABLE NINA AMOS April 22, 1917, in Pittsylvania Co., Virginia. Mable was born Jan. 17, 1898, in Pittsylvania Co., Virginia.

Mable was the daughter of W.R. Amos and Annie Leftwich Amos, according to the family Bible of John Henry Crider, her husband.

Children of JOHN CRIDER and MABLE AMOS are:

    i. MYRTLE LORANE7 CRIDER, b. March 14, 1918, Pittsylvania Co., Virginia.

    ii. JAMES HAYWOOD CRIDER, b. May 13, 1923, Pittsylvania Co., Virginia.

    iii. VIRGINIA ARLEEN CRIDER, b. March 18, 1925, Pittsylvania Co., Virginia.

    iv. CARLTON AMOS CRIDER, b. August 31, 1927, Pittsylvania Co., Virginia.

    v. RACHEL PATRICIA CRIDER, b. September 22, 1930, Pittsylvania Co., Virginia.

    vi. ONYX GROVE CRIDER, b. June 10, 1931, Pittsylvania Co., Virginia; d. May 1953, Pittsylvania Co., Virginia.

    vii. PHYLLIS JEAN CRIDER, b. May 3, 1933, Pittsylvania Co., Virginia.

    viii. VIRGIL DEAN CRIDER, b. March 14, 1938, Pittsylvania Co., Virginia.

100. ANGELINE J.6 CRIDER *(JAMES A.5, DAVID4, GEORGE3, DANIEL2 KRIDER, JOHN MICHAEL1 KREIDER)* was born in 1855 in Calloway Co., Kentucky, and died in 1922.

♥ Angeline married WILLIAM WARD in Weakley Co., Tennessee.

Children of ANGELINE CRIDER and WILLIAM WARD are:

    i.   MONTROSE7 WARD.
   ii. BEULAH WARD, m. BOYCE OLIVER.

101. EMMOGENE ANITA6 CRIDER *(JAMES WINSLOW5, THOMAS BENNETT4, GEORGE3, DANIEL2 KRIDER, JOHN MICHAEL1 KREIDER)* was born March 5, 1902, in Bradford, Gibson Co., Tennessee, and died July 19, 1992, in Corinth, Alcorn Co., Mississippi.

♥ Anita married HUBERT CIRSON JONES November 1, 1926, in Jackson, Hinds Co., Mississippi, son of SAMUEL JONES and FLORENCE SORRELL. Buried September, 1957, Corinth, Alcorn Co., Mississippi.

Anita taught music before her marriage to Hubert. She obtained her education at Synogogical College in Holly Springs, Mississippi. In addition, she attended summer sessions at the Bush Conservatory of Music in Chicago, Illinois, and the Cincinnati Conservatory in Ohio. Her first teaching position was as a music and gym teacher in Athens, Alabama. Her second position was in Friendship, Tennessee. Hubert was a senior in high school and her pupil, five years her junior. Despite the teasing questions of her daughters, she wouldn't offer the details of their courtship! They did not marry until Hubert was 21 years old, after which Anita stopped teaching. Hubert had several short careers before he purchased a furniture factory he named the Corinth Manufacturing Company. Also he enjoyed designing the furniture his company made. Their home was filled with beautiful wood furniture.

About his six daughters, Hubert used to tell people they were "cheaper by the dozen."

They were happily married until his death of heart failure at the age of 52.

Anita died peacefully in the Alcorn County Care-Inn nursing home at the age of 90. She was tired and ready to move on to a higher place.

Children of ANITA CRIDER and HUBERT JONES are:

129.   i.   EMMOGENE CRIDER7 JONES, b. December 25, 1927, Corinth, Alcorn Co., Mississippi.
130.   ii.   GLORIA MAY JONES, b. May 22, 1931, Corinth, Alcorn Co., Mississippi.
131.   iii.   CHRISTINE JOYCE JONES, b. June 23, 1932, Corinth, Alcorn Co., Mississippi.
132.   iv.   JESSE ANNA JONES, b. November 6, 1938, Corinth, Alcorn Co., Mississippi.
133.   v.   BEVERLY SUE JONES, b. March 4, 1940, Corinth, Alcorn Co., Mississippi.
134.   vi.   CHARLOTTE MARIE JONES, b. November 2, 1941, Corinth, Alcorn Co., Mississippi.

102. LONZO WELDON6 CRIDER *(PRESTON COLUMBUS5, DANIEL BENNETT4, GEORGE3, DANIEL2 KRIDER, JOHN MICHAEL1 KREIDER)* was born October 8, 1871, in Gibson Co., Tennessee, and died March 12, 1940, in Gibson Co., Tennessee. Buried at Bradford Cem., Gibson Co., Tennessee

Lonzo was the second Postmaster in Skullbone, Gibson County.

♥ Lonzo married KATE WILLIAMS in Gibson Co., Tennessee. Kate was born April 26, 1876, in Gibson Co., Tennessee, and died May 25, 1943, in Gibson Co., Tennessee. She was buried at Bradford Cem., Gibson Co., Tennessee.

Child of LONZO CRIDER and KATE WILLIAMS is:

    i. MILDRED FRANCES7 CRIDER, b. February 23, 1918, Gibson Co., Tennessee; m. T. C. COLLIE.

103. ADA FLORENCE6 CRIDER *(PRESTON COLUMBUS5, DANIEL BENNETT4, GEORGE3, DANIEL2 KRIDER, JOHN MICHAEL1 KREIDER)* was born August 23, 1873, in Bradford, Gibson Co., Tennessee, and died March 1, 1962, in Milan, Gibson Co., Tennessee.

♥ Ada married WILLIAM ANDERSON CAMPBELL September 6, 1891, in Gibson Co., Tennessee.

Child of ADA CRIDER and WILLIAM CAMPBELL is:

135.   i. HENRY ANANIAS7 CAMPBELL, b. May 27, 1901, Skullbone, Gibson Co., Tennessee; d. May 12, 1990, Albuquerque, Bernalillo Co., New Mexico.

104. JOHN WESLEY6 CRIDER *(MILTON E.5, GEORGE W.4, GEORGE3, DANIEL2 KRIDER, JOHN MICHAEL1 KREIDER)* was born July 8, 1869, in Calloway Co., Kentucky.

♥ John married IZORA FANETTA AUSTIN December 24, 1890, in Graves Co., Kentucky.

Children of JOHN CRIDER and IZORA AUSTIN are:

    i. VIRGIL7 CRIDER, b. March 31, 1896, Weakley Co., Tennessee.

    ii.   MAUDIE CRIDER, b. March 16, 1902, Weakley Co.,
         Tennessee.
   iii.   EUNICE CRIDER, b. June 13, 1905, Weakley Co., Tennessee.
   iv.   ROY CRIDER, b. July 12, 1909, Weakley Co., Tennessee.
    v.   BEATIE CRIDER, b. July 21, 1911, Weakley Co., Tennessee.

105. RICHARD ALBERT6 CRIDER *(FELIX HENRY5, RICHARD HENRY4, HENRY3, DANIEL2 KRIDER, JOHN MICHAEL1 KREIDER)* was born July 2, 1877, in Palmer Shelter, Carroll Co., Tennessee, and died October 23, 1952, in Carroll Co., Tennessee.

♥ Richard married MARY MORGAN February 2, 1900 in Carroll Co., Tennessee.

   Children of RICHARD CRIDER and MARY MORGAN are:

136.   i.   MAE7 CRIDER, b. June 17, 1901, Palmer Shelter, Carroll Co., Tennessee; d. June 30, 1983, Carroll Co., Tennessee.
137.   ii.   GRAYDON CARMACK CRIDER, b. September 13, 1903, Palmer Shelter, Carroll Co., Tennessee; d. December 8, 1985.
138.   iii.   ORVILLE CRIDER, b. November 2, 1905, Palmer Shelter, Carroll Co., Tennessee.
       iv.   IDA CRIDER, b. September 24, 1909, Palmer Shelter, Carroll Co., Tennessee; d. April 11, 1977, Carroll Co., Tennessee; m. NATHAN MEBANE.

           Ida Crider Mebane served as Clerk and Master of Carroll Co. Chancery Court for 25 years.

139.   v.   LILLIAN CRIDER, b. July 24, 1914, Palmer Shelter, Carroll Co., Tennessee.
140.   vi.   ROY ALBERT CRIDER, b. May 21, 1921, Palmer Shelter, Carroll Co., Tennessee; d. May 23, 1980, Carroll Co., Tennessee.

106. JOSIE NEVADA6 CRIDER *(FELIX HENRY5, RICHARD HENRY4, HENRY3, DANIEL2 KRIDER, JOHN MICHAEL1 KREIDER)* was born August 10, 1881, in Carroll Co., Tennessee, and died May 6, 1966, in Perry Co., Tennessee.

♥ Josie married CARLIE B. HOLLADAY November 27, 1904, in Carroll Co., Tennessee, son of ALLEN HOLLADAY and SARAH UTLEY. Carlie was born Sept. 30, 1882 in Benton Co., Tennessee, and died Jan. 24, 1965, at Perry Co., Tennessee.

Children of JOSIE CRIDER and CARLIE HOLLADAY are:

   i. RUTH MARIE7 HOLLADAY, b. October 26, 1905, Carroll Co., Tennessee.
   ii. JAMES ALLEN HOLLADAY, b. June 22, 1907, Carroll Co., Tennessee.
   iii. RICHARD AUDIE HOLLADAY, b. December 15, 1908, Carroll Co., Tennessee.
   iv. BENNIE ROBERT HOLLADAY, b. December 22, 1910, Carroll Co., Tennessee.
   v. EFFIE ROBERTA HOLLADAY, b. February 16, 1913, Carroll Co., Tennessee.
   vi. ALVIS MILTON HOLLADAY, b. January 19, 1915, Carroll Co., Tennessee.

   Alvis Milton Holladay is the author of an excellent book entitled "The HOLLADAY Family," published in 1983. It is available from the LDS Library on microfiche and is highly recommended reading for any and all descendants of Henry Crider and Permelia Lee.

   vii. GEORGIA NAOMI HOLLADAY, b. July 11, 1917, Carroll Co., Tennessee.

viii. BERTIE LEON HOLLADAY, b. July 7, 1919, Carroll Co., Tennessee.

ix. JOSIE MAEDENE HOLLADAY, b. March 24, 1921, Carroll Co., Tennessee.

x. CLAYTON BASIL HOLLADAY, b. March 27, 1923, Carroll Co., Tennessee.

xi. WENDELL GENE HOLLADAY, b. August 23, 1925, Carroll Co., Tennessee.

xii. SUE HELEN HOLLADAY, b. February 2, 1928, Carroll Co., Tennessee.

107. CARLIE B.6 HOLLADAY *(ALLEN5, CATHERINE4 CRIDER, HENRY3, DANIEL2 KRIDER, JOHN MICHAEL1 KREIDER)* was born September 30, 1882, in Benton Co., Tennessee, and died January 24, 1965, in Perry Co., Tennessee.

♥ Carlie married his cousin, JOSIE NEVADA CRIDER (see above), November 27, 1904, in Carroll Co., Tennessee, daughter of FELIX CRIDER and LARCENIA LAYCOOK.

Children of CARLIE HOLLADAY and JOSIE CRIDER are listed above.

108. HOMER LEE6 CRIDER *(ROBERT MONROE5, JAMES CARROLL4, HENRY3, DANIEL2 KRIDER, JOHN MICHAEL1 KREIDER)* was born 1903 in Carroll Co., Tennessee, and died 1960 in Carroll Co., Tennessee.

♥ Homer married ETHEL DUNN Bef. 1905 in Carroll Co., Tennessee.

Children of HOMER CRIDER and ETHEL DUNN are:

141.   i.   ROYAL DESMOND7 CRIDER, b. 1922, Dollar Hill Com.,
             Carroll Co., Tennessee.
142.   ii.   HELEN CRIDER, b. 1925, Carroll Co., Tennessee.
143.   iii. MARILYN CRIDER, b. 1929, Carroll Co., Tennessee.
144.   iv.   HOMER DUNN CRIDER, b. 1936, Carroll Co., Tennessee.
145.   v.   RICHARD ARLIN CRIDER, b. 1939, Carroll Co., Tennessee.

SEVENTH GENERATION

109. FRANCIS NEWTON7 CRIDER *(ALLEN TOM6, JOHN HENRY5, HENRY4, DANIEL3, DANIEL2 KRIDER, JOHN MICHAEL1 KREIDER)* was born February 25, 1863, in Crittenden Co., Kentucky, and died January 11, 1942, in Mesa Co., Colorado.

♥ Francis married ALICE BELLE FRALICK May 25, 1883, in Piney Fork, Crittenden Co., Kentucky. Alice was born Oct. 26, 1865, in Marion, Crittenden Co., Kentucky, and died March 14, 1948, at Meso Co., Colorado.

Child of FRANCIS CRIDER and ALICE FRALICK is:

    i.   JOHN ALLEN8 CRIDER, b. September 25, 1883, Marion, Crittenden Co., Kentucky; d. April 18, 1972, Grand Junction, Mesa Co., Colorado; m. DELLA MOORE, September 25, 1912, Phillips Co., Kansas.

110. GEORGE VERNON7 CRIDER *(WILLIAM H.6, JOHN HENRY5, HENRY4, DANIEL3, DANIEL2 KRIDER, JOHN MICHAEL1 KREIDER)* was born May 6, 1877, in Princeton, Caldwell Co., Kentucky, and died in 1956.

♥ George married MARTHA ANN HILLYARD October 14, 1903 in Phillips Co., Kansas. Martha was born Dec. 29, 1882, in Flatrock, Kentucky, and died Mar. 2, 1962, at Ault, Weld Co., Colorado.

Child of GEORGE CRIDER and MARTHA HILLYARD is:

     i.   RUTH FERN8 CRIDER, b. October 11, 1904, Phillips Co., Kansas; m. WALTER EUGENE DRAKE, July 15, 1930.

111. EMMETT COOPER7 CRIDER *(ZACHARIAH JOHNSON6, JACOB EWING5, JACOB B.4, JACOB3, DANIEL2 KRIDER, JOHN MICHAEL1 KREIDER)* was born in 1908 in Caldwell Co., Kentucky, and died in 1967.

Emmett attended Swarthmore College in Pennsylvania as well as the University of Kentucky. He served in the Navy during WWII.

♥ Emmett married SARA FRANCES AKIN in 1940 in Caldwell Co., Kentucky.

    Children of EMMETT CRIDER and SARA AKIN are:

146.   i.   ROBERT COOPER8 CRIDER, b. 1943, Caldwell Co., Kentucky.
147.   ii. SUZANNE CRIDER, b. 1946, Caldwell Co., Kentucky.

112. ZACHARIAH JOHNSON7 CRIDER III *(ZACHARIAH JOHNSON6, JACOB EWING5, JACOB B.4, JACOB3, DANIEL2 KRIDER, JOHN MICHAEL1 KREIDER)* was born in 1911 in Caldwell Co., Kentucky, and died in 1972.

Zachariah attended the University of Kentucky and was a civil engineer.

♥ Zachariah married MARY HELEN RANDOLPH in 1934 in Caldwell Co., Kentucky.

Children of ZACHARIAH CRIDER and MARY RANDOLPH are:

148.   i.   CYNTHIA KAY8 CRIDER, b. 1936, Caldwell Co., Kentucky.
        ii. JACKIE WAYNE CRIDER, b. 1942, Caldwell Co., Kentucky.

            Jackie attended Murray State University on a football scholarship.

149.   iii. JAMES RANDOLPH CRIDER, b. 1943, Caldwell Co., Kentucky; d. 1978.

113. ALICE7 CRIDER *(ZACHARIAH JOHNSON6, JACOB EWING5, JACOB B.4, JACOB3, DANIEL2 KRIDER, JOHN MICHAEL1 KREIDER)* was born in 1914 in Caldwell Co., Kentucky.

♥ Alice married JOSEPH BRADLEY LYKINS in 1944.

    Children of ALICE CRIDER and JOSEPH LYKINS are:

        i.   MELINDA LOU8 LYKINS, b. 1945; m. KEITH WOOD in 1978.
150.   ii. SANDRA JO LYKINS, b. 1946.
151.   iii. JOSEPH BRADLEY LYKINS , JR., b. 1951.

114. NELL7 CRIDER *(ZACHARIAH JOHNSON6, JACOB EWING5, JACOB B.4, JACOB3, DANIEL2 KRIDER, JOHN MICHAEL1 KREIDER)* was born 1914 in Caldwell Co., Kentucky.

♥ Nell married WILLIAM DUKE FOWLER Bef. 1938 in Caldwell Co., Kentucky.

    Child of NELL CRIDER and WILLIAM FOWLER is:

152.   i.   GWENDOLYN8 FOWLER, b. 1938.

115. JANE7 CRIDER *(ZACHARIAH JOHNSON6, JACOB EWING5, JACOB B.4, JACOB3, DANIEL2 KRIDER, JOHN MICHAEL1 KREIDER)* was born in 1922 in Caldwell Co., Kentucky, and died in 1980.

♥ Jane married IRVING B. MONTAGUE.

Children of JANE CRIDER and IRVING MONTAGUE are:

    i.   MARCELLA8 MONTAGUE.
    ii. DIANA MONTAGUE.
    iii. BARRY MONTAGUE.

116. DAISY FRANCES7 CRIDER *(MILTON BIRD6, WILLIAM BRADLEY5, WILLIAM M.4, JACOB3, DANIEL2 KRIDER, JOHN MICHAEL1 KREIDER)* was born October 19, 1903, in Marshall, Saline Co., Missouri.

♥ Daisy married NOVEL CAMPBELL June 23, 1921, in Marshall, Saline Co., Missouri. Novel was born Mar. 22, 1899, and died July 8, 1949, in Poteau, Le Flore Co., Oklahoma.

Children of DAISY CRIDER and NOVEL CAMPBELL are:

153.   i.   NOVELINE FRANCES8 CAMPBELL, b. May 10, 1926.
154.   ii. ROBY MAE CAMPBELL, b. February 22, 1928.

Daisy married secondly J. Ervine Clements, Sr., the father of her son-in-law.

117. MILTON R.7 CRIDER *(MILTON BIRD6, WILLIAM BRADLEY5, WILLIAM M.4, JACOB3, DANIEL2 KRIDER, JOHN MICHAEL1 KREIDER)* was born September 29, 1905, in Marshall, Saline Co., Missouri.

♥ Milton married GLADYS MAE CATES June 6, 1936, in Kansas City, Jackson Co., Missouri. Gladys was born Dec. 8, 1909, in St. Joseph, Buchanan Co., Missouri.

Children of MILTON CRIDER and GLADYS CATES are:

155.   i.   DONNA RHEA8 CRIDER, b. March 25, 1937, Kansas City, Jackson Co., Missouri.
156.   ii. KAY LAVONNE CRIDER, b. January 26, 1940, Kansas City, Jackson Co., Missouri.

118. JOSEPH BALLENTINE7 CRIDER *(MILTON BIRD6, WILLIAM BRADLEY5, WILLIAM M.4, JACOB3, DANIEL2 KRIDER, JOHN MICHAEL1 KREIDER)* was born December 19, 1911, in Marshall, Saline Co., Missouri, and died August 28, 1967, in Jonesboro, Craighead Co., Arkansas.

♥ Joseph married ELAINE VIOLA NOWAK August 28, 1936, in Marshall, Saline Co., Missouri.

Child of JOSEPH CRIDER and ELAINE NOWAK is:

157.   i.   BEVERLY JEAN8 CRIDER, b. November 6, 1937, Marshall, Saline Co., Missouri.

119. FOSTER KEVIL7 CRIDER *(ALBERT FOSTER6, WILLIAM BRADLEY5, WILLIAM M.4, JACOB3, DANIEL2 KRIDER, JOHN MICHAEL1 KREIDER)* was born March 3, 1907.

♥ Foster married HELEN POWERS July 20, 1935.

Children of FOSTER CRIDER and HELEN POWERS are:

     i.   JANE RHEE8 CRIDER.
     ii. THOMAS KEVIL CRIDER.
    iii. DOROTHY HELEN CRIDER.

120. NOEL MONTGOMERY7 CRIDER *(ALBERT FOSTER6, WILLIAM BRADLEY5, WILLIAM M.4, JACOB3, DANIEL2 KRIDER, JOHN MICHAEL1 KREIDER)* was born December 25, 1908.

♥ Noel married SAMUEL C. MURRAY February 13, 1926.

Children of NOEL CRIDER and SAMUEL MURRAY are:

     i.   NOEL8 MURRAY.
     ii. SAMUEL CURTIS MURRAY.

121. HUBERT DIXON7 CRIDER *(LAWRENCE EDWIN6, WILLIAM BRADLEY5, WILLIAM M.4, JACOB3, DANIEL2 KRIDER, JOHN MICHAEL1 KREIDER)* was born January 21, 1903, in Marion, Crittenden Co., Kentucky.

♥ Hubert married FLORENCE BENNETT in Crittenden Co., Kentucky.

Children of HUBERT CRIDER and FLORENCE BENNETT are:

    i.   CAROLYN M.8 CRIDER, b. December 10, 1929, Marion,
         Crittenden Co., Kentucky.
   ii.   LAWRENCE EDWIN CRIDER, b. February 17, 1941, Marion,
         Crittenden Co., Kentucky.
  iii.   ANDREA MELISSA CRIDER, b. February 3, 1944, Marion,
         Crittenden Co., Kentucky.

122. MARTHA VIRGINIA7 CRIDER *(LAWRENCE EDWIN6, WILLIAM BRADLEY5, WILLIAM M.4, JACOB3, DANIEL2 KRIDER, JOHN MICHAEL1 KREIDER)* was born April 3, 1911, in Marion, Crittenden Co., Kentucky.

♥ Martha married JAMES W. KING in Crittenden Co., Kentucky. James was born May 7, 1904, in Crittenden Co., Kentucky, and died May 16, 1974, at Maryville, Blount Co., Tennessee. Buried at Grandview Cem., Maryville, Blount Co., Tennessee.

Children of MARTHA CRIDER and JAMES KING are:

         i.   JOHN HILL8 KING, b. July 22, 1934, Maryville, Blount Co.,
              Tennessee; m. JANET GREEN.
158.   ii.   JAMES EDWIN KING, b. July 14, 1938, Maryville, Blount Co.,
              Tennessee.
159.   iii.   MARCIA A. KING, b. January 6, 1944, Maryville, Blount Co.,
              Tennessee.

123. ALBERT THOMPSON7 CRIDER *(JACOB HUGHEY6, WILLIAM BRADLEY5, WILLIAM M.4, JACOB3, DANIEL2 KRIDER, JOHN MICHAEL1 KREIDER)* was born December 22, 1909, in Marion, Crittenden Co., Kentucky.

♥ Albert married VIOLA WINDERS June 22, 1935, in Crittenden Co., Kentucky.

Children of ALBERT CRIDER and VIOLA WINDERS are:

    i.   THOMAS EDWIN8 CRIDER, b. Abt. 1937, Crittenden Co., Kentucky.
    ii. MARTHA J. CRIDER, b. Abt. 1939, Crittenden Co., Kentucky.
    iii. BILLY JOE CRIDER, b. Abt. 1941, Crittenden Co., Kentucky.
    iv. ALBERT MICHAEL CRIDER, b. Abt. 1943, Crittenden Co., Kentucky.

124. WILLIAM EDWIN7 CRIDER *(JACOB HUGHEY6, WILLIAM BRADLEY5, WILLIAM M.4, JACOB3, DANIEL2 KRIDER, JOHN MICHAEL1 KREIDER)* was born December 12, 1917, in Marion, Crittenden Co., Kentucky.

♥ William married ERMA KENDALL June 29, 1958, in Crittenden Co., Kentucky.

Child of WILLIAM CRIDER and ERMA KENDALL is:

    i.   MARK ALLEN8 CRIDER, b. Abt. 1960, Crittenden Co., Kentucky.

Crider Families of Virginia, Kentucky and Tennessee

125. SARAH JANETTE7 CRIDER *(JACOB HUGHEY6, WILLIAM BRADLEY5, WILLIAM M.4, JACOB3, DANIEL2 KRIDER, JOHN MICHAEL1 KREIDER)* was born September 5, 1921, in Crittenden Co., Kentucky.

♥ Sarah married KENYAN LEISHMAN.

Children of SARAH CRIDER and KENYAN LEISHMAN are:

    i. JANE KENYAN8 LEISHMAN.
    ii. RUTH VIRGINIA LEISHMAN.
    iii. MARTHA LEISHMAN.

126. NORMAN J.7 CRIDER *(HOMER EVERETTE6, DAVIS EWING5, WILLIAM M.4, JACOB3, DANIEL2 KRIDER, JOHN MICHAEL1 KREIDER)* was born March 16, 1892, in Crittenden Co., Kentucky, and died August 4, 1973, in Crittenden Co., Kentucky.

♥ Norman married MARGE KIRK Bef. 1951 in Crittenden Co., Kentucky. Marge was born Oct. 3, 1912, in Crittenden Co., Kentucky.

Children of NORMAN CRIDER and MARGE KIRK are:

    i. JAMES DUANE8 CRIDER, b. July 21, 1951, Crittenden Co., Kentucky.
    ii. CHRISTOPHER VANCE CRIDER, b. August 24, 1962, Countryside, Chicago, Illinois; m. MARY SUSAN ENGLISH, August 29, 1986, Illinois.

127. WALLACE7 CRIDER *(WALLACE MCKINLEY6, DAVIS EWING5, WILLIAM M.4, JACOB3, DANIEL2 KRIDER, JOHN MICHAEL1 KREIDER)* was born October 29, 1935, in Mott City, Crittenden Co., Kentucky, and died April 4, 1987, in Crittenden Co., Kentucky. Buried at Crayne Cemetery, Marion, Crittenden Co., Kentucky

♥ Wallace married FAY CAROL JACKSON August 26, 1966, in Crittenden Co., Kentucky. Fay was born Jan. 19, 1942, in Muhlenberg Co., Kentucky.

Child of WALLACE CRIDER and FAY JACKSON is:

    i.   MARY ELIZABETH8 CRIDER, b. April 4, 1967, Livingston Co., Kentucky.

128. CLYDE BENNETT7 EAST *(MARY ELIZABETH6 CRIDER, GEORGE DAVID5, DAVID4, JOHN3, DANIEL2 KRIDER, JOHN MICHAEL1 KREIDER)* was born July 19, 1921, in Coles Hill, Pittsylvania Co., Virginia.

Clyde B. East has contributed the information on the descendants of George D. Crider and Lucy Jacobs.

♥ Clyde married MARGARET ANN DILKS August 12, 1944. Margaret was born July 26, 1923, in Hamilton, Wentworth, Ontario, Canada.

Margaret is the daughter of Charles Edward Dilks of Cirencester, Gloucestershire, England and Isabella Selina Burton Dilks of Virginia, Ontario, Canada.

Child of CLYDE EAST and MARGARET DILKS is:

    i.   PENELOPE ANN8 EAST, b. August 1, 1952, Sumter, Sumter Co., South Carolina; m. LAWRENCE CHARLES ROSS.

Penny Ross contributed information on the descendants of George D. Crider and Lucy Jacobs.

129. EMMOGENE CRIDER7 JONES *(EMMOGENE ANITA6 CRIDER, JAMES WINSLOW5, THOMAS BENNETT4, GEORGE3, DANIEL2 KRIDER, JOHN MICHAEL1 KREIDER)* was born December 25, 1927, in Corinth, Alcorn Co., Mississippi.

♥ Gene married VERNON HECHT BOYD , JR. May 30, 1953 in Richmond, Henrico Co., Virginia. Birth date: Jan 25, 1918. He died in Richmond, Virginia, in June, 1988, of a heart attack.

Children of EMMOGENE JONES and VERNON BOYD are:

160.   i.   SUSAN THERESE8 BOYD, b. September 11, 1958, Richmond, Henrico Co., Virginia.
         ii.   KATHRYN PAGE BOYD, b. June 10, 1962, Richmond, Henrico Co., Virginia; m. DAVID EARL BAILEY, May 19, 1990, Richmond, Henrico Co., Virginia.
       iii.   VERNON RANDOLPH BOYD, b. October 9, 1963, Richmond, Henrico Co., Virginia; m. GEORGANN MCGRUDER, May 6, 1989, Richmond, Henrico Co., Virginia.

130. GLORIA MAY7 JONES *(EMMOGENE ANITA6 CRIDER, JAMES WINSLOW5, THOMAS BENNETT4, GEORGE3, DANIEL2 KRIDER, JOHN MICHAEL1 KREIDER)* was born May 22, 1931, in Corinth, Alcorn Co., Mississippi. Christened: August 30, 1931, Corinth, Alcorn Co., Mississippi.

♥ Gloria married HERBERT GEORGE KRIEGELZ June 2, 1956, in Corinth, Alcorn Co., Mississippi. Herb was born Jan. 10, 1922, in Tigerton, Shawano Co., Wisconsin.

Herb is the son of George Richard Kriegel and Alvina Augusta Amanda Kohn Kriegel.

Children of GLORIA JONES and HERBERT KRIEGEL are:

161.   i.   JAY HERBERT8 KRIEGEL, b. April 28, 1958, Corydon, Harrison Co., Indiana.

       ii. JOHN PETER KRIEGEL, b. May 11, 1960, Birmingham, Jefferson Co., Alabama; d. May 12, 1960, Birmingham, Jefferson Co., Alabama.

           John was born prematurely and survived but one day. He is buried atop his grandfather, H.C. Jones, in Corinth, Mississippi. Christened: May 11, 1960, Birmingham, Jefferson Co., Alabama Buried: May 14, 1960, Corinth, Alcorn Co., Mississippi.

      iii. KATHRYN ANNA KRIEGEL, b. June 22, 1961, Hattiesburg, Forest Co., Mississippi; d. July 29, 1964, Birmingham, Jefferson Co., Alabama.

           Kathryn died of a brain tumor at the tender age of three years. Christened: August 6, 1961, Hattiesburg, Forest Co., Mississippi Buried: July 31, 1964, Birmingham, Jefferson Co., Alabama.

iv.DAVID GEORGE KRIEGEL, b. January 4, 1964, Birmingham, Jefferson Co., Alabama; christened: March 20, 1964, Birmingham, Jefferson Co., Alabama m. PAMELA ANN STEESE, September 9, 1989, Doraville, DeKalb Co., Georgia.

           David graduated from the University of Georgia in June, 1986, with a Bachelor of Music and continued to earn a Master's in June, 1991, both in Classical Guitar, Performance.

He began doctoral studies in Music/Guitar in January, 1993, at Arizona State University.

Pamela is the daughter of John Palm Steese and Joan Marie Schuman Steese. Pam graduated from Georgia State University in December, 1989, with a major in Spanish Literature and a minor in French.

131. CHRISTINE JOYCE7 JONES *(EMMOGENE ANITA6 CRIDER, JAMES WINSLOW5, THOMAS BENNETT4, GEORGE3, DANIEL2 KRIDER, JOHN MICHAEL1 KREIDER)* was born June 23, 1932, in Corinth, Alcorn Co., Mississippi.

Christine was raised in Corinth, Mississippi as the third of six daughters. She went to Judson College for one year where she met E.V. Smith (he was attending a nearby military academy). After her marriage, she attended Indiana University in Bloomington, majoring in Home Economics, until her first child was born.

Christine has been employed by the City of Dayton, Ohio, for many years. She is currently (1997) employed in the Office of Redevelopment where she purchases new properties for the city.

♥ Christine married (1) E. VERNON SMITH June 14, 1951 in Columbus, Lownes Co., Mississippi, son of ELMER V. SMITH and HAZEL BUNDY. Born May 14, 1932, in Gary, Indiana.

E.V. graduated from Indiana University as a Distinguished Military Graduate in1954, majoring in Accounting. He began his military career as a Lieutenant, serving as a paratrooper in the 82nd Airborne Division and in Korea (1956). He resigned from active service in 1959, continuing to serve in the Army Reserves. He retired as a Major.

His hobbies revolve around music and history. E.V. plays the trumpet in the Richmond (Virginia) Concert Band. His interest in the Civil War has kept him busy collecting relics and researching. He is a co-author of *"Rio Hill: Happenings and Relics"* (Battle in Charlottesville, Virginia in 1864).

Children of CHRISTINE JONES and E.V. SMITH are:

162.　　i.　REBECCA LYNN (SMITH)8 BLACKWELL, b. July 21, 1952, Corinth, Alcorn Co., Mississippi.
163.　　ii.　CLAY BLACKWELL SMITH, b. February 25, 1956, Ft. Bragg, Cumberland Co., North Carolina.

♥ Christine married (2) HENRI MARECHAL in 1962 in Indianapolis, Indiana. Henri was born in Brussels, Belgium.

Child of CHRISTINE JONES and HENRI MARECHAL is:

　　　iii.　BEVERLEE RENEE8 MARECHAL, b. November 19, 1962, Columbus, Franklin Co., Ohio.

　　　Beverlee graduated from Ohio State University with a degree in Wildlife Management. She currently (1997) works with the U.S. Department of Fish and Wildlife Management in San Diego, California.

♥ Christine married (3) EDWIN ROE in 1975 in Dayton, Montgomery Co., Ohio. Ed was born Nov. 4, 1918 and died in July, 1980, in Dayton, Montgomery Co., Ohio.

132. JESSE ANNA7 JONES *(EMMOGENE ANITA6 CRIDER, JAMES WINSLOW5, THOMAS BENNETT4, GEORGE3, DANIEL2 KRIDER, JOHN MICHAEL1 KREIDER)* was born November 6, 1938, in Corinth, Alcorn Co., Mississippi.

♥ Jesse married MILTON B. GRAY December 8, 1959, in Mississippi.

Children of JESSE JONES and MILTON GRAY are:

164.   i.   DONNA LYNN8 GRAY, b. August 1, 1961, Corinth, Alcorn
           Co., Mississippi.
      ii.   ANITA DALE GRAY, b. October 17, 1963, Corinth, Alcorn
           Co., Mississippi; m. ROBBIE LEROY TRUSSELL, November
           30, 1985, Gulfport, Harrison Co., Mississippi.

           Robbie is the son of Byrd James Trussell and Mary Scarberry
           Trussell.

133. BEVERLY SUE7 JONES *(EMMOGENE ANITA6 CRIDER, JAMES
WINSLOW5, THOMAS BENNETT4, GEORGE3, DANIEL2 KRIDER, JOHN
MICHAEL1 KREIDER)* was born March 4, 1940, in Corinth, Alcorn Co.,
Mississippi

♥ Beverly married LOUIS MARTIN JETER July 7, 1963 in Memphis,
Shelby Co., Tennessee. Louis was born Sept. 22, 1935, in Covington,
Tipton Co., Tennessee.

Louis is a graduate of Murray State College in Murray, Kentucky. He is
the son of Louis Martin Jeter, Sr., and Grace Wheeler Cobb of
Covington, Tennessee.

Children of BEVERLY JONES and LOUIS JETER are:

      i.   JILL CURRIE8 JETER, b. October 10, 1966, Nashville,
          Davidson Co., Tennessee.

ii.   ANDREW COBB JETER, b. March 25, 1973, Nashville, Davidson Co., Tennessee.

134. CHARLOTTE MARIE7 JONES *(EMMOGENE ANITA6 CRIDER, JAMES WINSLOW5, THOMAS BENNETT4, GEORGE3, DANIEL2 KRIDER, JOHN MICHAEL1 KREIDER)* was born November 2, 1941, in Corinth, Alcorn Co., Mississippi.

Child of CHARLOTTE MARIE JONES is:

165.   i.   CONSTANCE JUANITA8 JONES, b. January 24, 1961, Corinth, Alcorn Co., Mississippi.

Child of CHARLOTTE MARIE JONES is:

            ii.   CHARLES LAMAR8 JONES, b. March 8, 1963, Corinth, Alcorn Co., Mississippi.

Charlotte's husband is Terry Latch.

135. HENRY ANANIAS7 CAMPBELL *(ADA FLORENCE6 CRIDER, PRESTON COLUMBUS5, DANIEL BENNETT4, GEORGE3, DANIEL2 KRIDER, JOHN MICHAEL1 KREIDER)* was born May 27, 1901, in Skullbone, Gibson Co., Tennessee, and died May 12, 1990, in Albuquerque, Bernalillo Co., New Mexico. Buried: May 14, 1990, Sunset Memorial, Albuquerque, Bernalillo Co., New Mexico

♥ Henry married UNA MAE DRAPER August 7, 1928, in Wauseon, Fulton Co., Ohio. Una was born Dec. 4, 1906, in Bingham, Lenawee Co., Michagan, and died July 22, 1978, in Albuquerque, Bernalillo Co..

She was buried at Sunset Memorial Cem., Albuquerque, Bernalillo Co., New Mexico

Children of HENRY CAMPBELL and UNA DRAPER are:

166.   i.   HENRIETTA GENE8 CAMPBELL, b. June 11, 1929, Lansing, Ingham Co., Michigan.
       ii.   ELOISE MARGARET CAMPBELL, b. July 23, 1930, Lansing, Ingham Co., Michigan; m. TED BRACKETT, November 7, 1950, Albuquerque, Bernalillo Co., New Mexico.

136. MAE7 CRIDER *(RICHARD ALBERT6, FELIX HENRY5, RICHARD HENRY4, HENRY3, DANIEL2 KRIDER, JOHN MICHAEL1 KREIDER)* was born June 17, 1901, in Palmer Shelter, Carroll Co., Tennessee, and died June 30, 1983, in Carroll Co., Tennessee.

Mae Crider White taught school for several years in Carroll Co.

♥   Mae married WILLIAM RAY WHITE Bef. 1926 in Carroll Co., Tennessee.

Children of MAE CRIDER and WILLIAM WHITE are:

       i.   WILLIAM RAY8 WHITE , JR., b. January 11, 1926, Carroll Co., Tennessee; d. October 23, 1984.
      ii.   MARIBELLE WHITE, b. January 3, 1929.
     iii.   IDA FAY WHITE, b. October 9, 1939.

137. GRAYDON CARMACK7 CRIDER *(RICHARD ALBERT6, FELIX HENRY5, RICHARD HENRY4, HENRY3, DANIEL2 KRIDER, JOHN*

*MICHAEL*1 *KREIDER)* was born September 13, 1903, in Palmer Shelter, Carroll Co., Tennessee, and died December 8, 1985.

Graydon was an attorney and served in the state legislature as a senator for several terms.

♥ Graydon married HALLIE ROWLAND Bef. 1928 in Tennessee.

Child of GRAYDON CRIDER and HALLIE ROWLAND is:

    i.   JAMES ALBERT8 CRIDER, b. May 12, 1928, Tennessee; d. August 1985.

        James served in the U.S. Navy and retired as a Lt. Commander.

138. ORVILLE7 CRIDER *(RICHARD ALBERT*6, *FELIX HENRY*5, *RICHARD HENRY*4, *HENRY*3, *DANIEL*2 *KRIDER, JOHN MICHAEL*1 *KREIDER)* was born November 2, 1905, in Palmer Shelter, Carroll Co., Tennessee.

♥ Orville married JAMES P. WYATT Bef. 1932.

Children of ORVILLE CRIDER and JAMES WYATT are:

    i.   JAMES CRIDER8 WYATT, b. April 6, 1932, Carroll Co., Tennessee.
    ii. ROY CARMACK WYATT, b. May 8, 1943, Carroll Co., Tennessee.

139. LILLIAN7 CRIDER *(RICHARD ALBERT6, FELIX HENRY5, RICHARD HENRY4, HENRY3, DANIEL2 KRIDER, JOHN MICHAEL1 KREIDER)* was born July 24, 1914, in Palmer Shelter, Carroll Co., Tennessee.

♥ Lillian married ALTON HOLLAND Bef. 1935 in Tennessee.

Children of LILLIAN CRIDER and ALTON HOLLAND are

    i. PATRICIA DAY8 HOLLAND, b. July 10, 1935.
    ii. GWEN HOLLAND, b. September 22, 1955.

140. ROY ALBERT7 CRIDER *(RICHARD ALBERT6, FELIX HENRY5, RICHARD HENRY4, HENRY3, DANIEL2 KRIDER, JOHN MICHAEL1 KREIDER)* was born May 21, 1921, in Palmer Shelter, Carroll Co., Tennessee, and died May 23, 1980, in Carroll Co., Tennessee.

Roy Albert Crider served as a first lieutenant in World War II.

♥ Roy married FAY MCALPINE Bef. 1953.

Children of ROY CRIDER and FAY MCALPINE are:

    i. RICHARD ALBERT8 CRIDER, b. July 19, 1953.
    ii. MARY CRIDER, b. October 4, 1954.

141. ROYAL DESMOND7 CRIDER *(HOMER LEE6, ROBERT MONROE5, JAMES CARROLL4, HENRY3, DANIEL2 KRIDER, JOHN MICHAEL1 KREIDER)* was born in 1922 in Dollar Hill, Carroll Co., Tennessee.

Desmond retired from the U.S. Postal Service with 35 years service in the Huntingdon post office. Also, he served as a pilot and B29 bombardier in WWII, retiring as a Major from the Air Force Reserves.

♥ Desmond married DORIS LEWELLING Bef. 1944 in Carroll Co., Tennessee.

Children of Royal Desmond CRIDER and DORIS LEWELLING are:

     i.   RANDALL BRIAN8 CRIDER, b. 1944.
    ii.   RUSSELL CRAIG CRIDER, b. 1948.
   iii.   GRETA LOU CRIDER, b. 1954.

142. HELEN7 CRIDER *(HOMER LEE6, ROBERT MONROE5, JAMES CARROLL4, HENRY3, DANIEL2 KRIDER, JOHN MICHAEL1 KREIDER)* was born in 1925 in Carroll Co., Tennessee.

♥ Helen married CLYDE MILAM Bef. 1950 in Tennessee.

Clyde is the son of Rice and Tweetie Milam of Clarksburg.

Children of HELEN CRIDER and CLYDE MILAM are:

     i.   STEVE8 MILAM, b. 1950, Tennessee.
    ii.   STAN MILAM, b. 1954, Tennessee.

143. MARILYN7 CRIDER *(HOMER LEE6, ROBERT MONROE5, JAMES CARROLL4, HENRY3, DANIEL2 KRIDER, JOHN MICHAEL1 KREIDER)* was born in 1929 in Carroll Co., Tennessee.

♥ Marilyn married LESLIE HILLIS Bef. 1958.

Leslie is the son of Thomas and Oma Lewis Hillis.

Children of MARILYN CRIDER and LESLIE HILLIS are:

> i. MARK8 HILLIS, b. 1958.
> ii. BETH HILLIS, b. 1961.
> iii. PATRICK HILLIS, b. 1964.

144. HOMER DUNN7 CRIDER *(HOMER LEE6, ROBERT MONROE5, JAMES CARROLL4, HENRY3, DANIEL2 KRIDER, JOHN MICHAEL1 KREIDER)* was born in 1936 in Carroll Co., Tennessee.

♥ Homer married JOYCE ESKEW Bef. 1957.

Joyce is the daughter of Everette and Florence Eskew.

Children of HOMER CRIDER and JOYCE ESKEW are:

> i. HAL8 CRIDER, b. 1957, Carroll Co., Tennessee.
> ii. HARLAN CRIDER, b. 1960, Carroll Co., Tennessee.

145. RICHARD ARLIN7 CRIDER *(HOMER LEE6, ROBERT MONROE5, JAMES CARROLL4, HENRY3, DANIEL2 KRIDER, JOHN MICHAEL1 KREIDER)* was born in 1939 in Carroll Co., Tennessee.

♥ Richard married MELODY BRUNDIGE Bef. 1968 in Tennessee.

Children of RICHARD CRIDER and MELODY BRUNDIGE are:

   i.   MICHAEL8 CRIDER, b. 1968, Tennessee.
  ii.   KATHY CRIDER, b. 1971, Tennessee.

EIGHTH GENERATION

146. ROBERT COOPER8 CRIDER *(EMMETT COOPER7, ZACHARIAH JOHNSON6, JACOB EWING5, JACOB B.4, JACOB3, DANIEL2 KRIDER, JOHN MICHAEL1 KREIDER)* was born in 1943 in Caldwell Co., Kentucky.

Robert is a graduate of Murray State University.

♥ Robert married REBECCA SMITH Bef. 1965 in Kentucky.

Children of ROBERT CRIDER and REBECCA SMITH are:

    i.   CAROLYN MARIE9 CRIDER, b. 1965.
    ii. JAMES COOPER CRIDER, b. 1967.
    iii. CLAUDE AKIN CRIDER, b. 1972.

147. SUZANNE8 CRIDER *(EMMETT COOPER7, ZACHARIAH JOHNSON6, JACOB EWING5, JACOB B.4, JACOB3, DANIEL2 KRIDER, JOHN MICHAEL1 KREIDER)* was born in 1946 in Caldwell Co., Kentucky.

Suzanne attended Murray State University and is a surgical technician.

♥ Suzanne married JESSE CHARLES BOLLINGER Bef. 1974 in Kentucky.

Children of SUZANNE CRIDER and JESSE BOLLINGER are:

    i.   JESSE CHARLES9 BOLLINGER, JR., b. 1974, Kentucky.

ii.   ANDREW PETER BOLLINGER, b. 1976, Kentucky.

148. CYNTHIA KAY8 CRIDER *(ZACHARIAH JOHNSON7, ZACHARIAH JOHNSON6, JACOB EWING5, JACOB B.4, JACOB3, DANIEL2 KRIDER, JOHN MICHAEL1 KREIDER)* was born in 1936 in Caldwell Co., Kentucky.

Cynthia graduated from Memphis State University and is employed as a teacher. She provided the information on the families and descendants of Jacob Crider and Mary Reitter in Caldwell County, Kentucky, in the heritage book of that county.

♥ Cynthia married RICHARD DALE WHITSETT in 1960 in Caldwell Co., Kentucky.

Children of CYNTHIA CRIDER and RICHARD WHITSETT are:

  i.   RICHARD BRADLEY9 WHITSETT, b. 1965.
  ii. MARY LOUISE WHITSETT, b. 1968.

149. JAMES RANDOLPH8 CRIDER *(ZACHARIAH JOHNSON7, ZACHARIAH JOHNSON6, JACOB EWING5, JACOB B.4, JACOB3, DANIEL2 KRIDER, JOHN MICHAEL1 KREIDER)* was born in 1943 in Caldwell Co., Kentucky, and died 1978.

James attended Murray State University in Kentucky.

♥ James married WANDA KAY HOLT in 1964 in Caldwell Co., Kentucky.

Children of JAMES CRIDER and WANDA HOLT are:

    i. JAMES RANDOLPH9 CRIDER , JR., b. 1965.
    ii. KEVIN MATTHEW CRIDER, b. 1974.

150. SANDRA JO8 LYKINS *(ALICE7 CRIDER, ZACHARIAH JOHNSON6, JACOB EWING5, JACOB B.*4, *JACOB*3, *DANIEL*2 *KRIDER, JOHN MICHAEL*1 *KREIDER)* was born 1946.

♥ Sandra married LARRY BIRDWELL 1966.

Children of SANDRA LYKINS and LARRY BIRDWELL are:

    i. CAROL9 BIRDWELL, b. 1967.
    ii. ROBIN BIRDWELL, b. 1972.

151. JOSEPH BRADLEY8 LYKINS , JR. *(ALICE7 CRIDER, ZACHARIAH JOHNSON6, JACOB EWING5, JACOB B.*4, *JACOB*3, *DANIEL*2 *KRIDER, JOHN MICHAEL*1 *KREIDER)* was born 1951.

♥ Joseph married PHOEBE CLURE Bef. 1977.

Children of JOSEPH LYKINS and PHOEBE CLURE are:

    i. MICHAEL9 LYKINS, b. 1977.
    ii. SUZANNE LYKINS, b. 1981.

152. GWENDOLYN8 FOWLER *(NELL7 CRIDER, ZACHARIAH JOHNSON6, JACOB EWING5, JACOB B.4, JACOB3, DANIEL2 KRIDER, JOHN MICHAEL1 KREIDER)* was born 1938.

♥ Gwendolyn married RAY JENNER 1957.

Children of GWENDOLYN FOWLER and RAY JENNER are:

    i.   DAVID RAY9 JENNER, b. 1961.
   ii.   RITA RAYE JENNER, b. 1963.
  iii.   JOHN RAY JENNER, b. 1965.

153. NOVELINE FRANCES8 CAMPBELL *(DAISY FRANCES7 CRIDER, MILTON BIRD6, WILLIAM BRADLEY5, WILLIAM M.4, JACOB3, DANIEL2 KRIDER, JOHN MICHAEL1 KREIDER)* was born May 10, 1926.

♥ Noveline married ROBERT HAYOB Bef. 1950.

Children of NOVELINE CAMPBELL and ROBERT HAYOB are:

    i.   KAREN9 HAYOB, b. December 13, 1950.
   ii.   KATHY HAYOB, b. December 26, 1951.

154. ROBY MAE8 CAMPBELL *(DAISY FRANCES7 CRIDER, MILTON BIRD6, WILLIAM BRADLEY5, WILLIAM M.4, JACOB3, DANIEL2 KRIDER, JOHN MICHAEL1 KREIDER)* was born February 22, 1928.

♥ Roby Mae married J. ERVINE CLEMENTS Bef. 1950.

Children of ROBY CAMPBELL and J. CLEMENTS are:

    i.   KERRY9 CLEMENTS, b. June 24, 1950.
   ii. KEVIN CLEMENTS, b. May 25, 1954.
  iii. AMY CLEMENTS, b. June 13, 1963.

155. DONNA RHEA8 CRIDER *(MILTON R.7, MILTON BIRD6, WILLIAM BRADLEY5, WILLIAM M.4, JACOB3, DANIEL2 KRIDER, JOHN MICHAEL1 KREIDER)* was born March 25, 1937, in Kansas City, Jackson Co., Missouri.

♥ Donna married (1) HAROLD SICKLES August 17, 1957, in Raytown, Jackson Co., Missouri.

Children of DONNA CRIDER and HAROLD SICKLES are:

    i.   STEVEN HAROLD9 SICKLES, b. July 9, 1959, Jackson Co., Missouri.
   ii. SHERRI RENEE SICKLES, b. September 11, 1960, Jackson Co., Missouri.

♥ Donna married (2) LELAND J. DEAN October 15, 1967, in Kansas City, Jackson Co., Missouri. Leland was born Nov. 28, 1931.

Child of DONNA CRIDER and LELAND DEAN is:

  iii. JULIE ANNA9 DEAN, b. November 3, 1969, Jackson Co., Missouri.

156. KAY LAVONNE8 CRIDER *(MILTON R.7, MILTON BIRD6, WILLIAM BRADLEY5, WILLIAM M.4, JACOB3, DANIEL2 KRIDER, JOHN MICHAEL1*

KREIDER) was born January 26, 1940, in Kansas City, Jackson Co., Missouri.

♥ Kay married ROBERT PATTON January 6, 1958, in Raytown, Jackson Co., Missouri. Robert was born Sept. 29, 1937.

Children of KAY CRIDER and ROBERT PATTON are:

    i.   MICHAEL EUGENE9 PATTON, b. November 10, 1960, Jackson Co., Missouri.
    ii. MARK RAE PATTON, b. November 26, 1961, Jackson Co., Missouri.
    iii. JANICE MARIE PATTON, b. September 28, 1963, Jackson Co., Missouri.
    iv. JO ANNA PATTON, b. June 4, 1965, Jackson Co., Missouri.

157. BEVERLY JEAN8 CRIDER *(JOSEPH BALLENTINE7, MILTON BIRD6, WILLIAM BRADLEY5, WILLIAM M.4, JACOB3, DANIEL2 KRIDER, JOHN MICHAEL1 KREIDER)* was born November 6, 1937, in Marshall, Saline Co., Missouri.

♥ Beverly married JACK OWENS Bef. 1958 in Missouri.

Children of BEVERLY CRIDER and JACK OWENS are:

    i.   MARTHA JO9 OWENS, b. February 11, 1958.
    ii. MARSHA JEAN OWENS, b. February 23, 1961.

158. JAMES EDWIN8 KING *(MARTHA VIRGINIA7 CRIDER, LAWRENCE EDWIN6, WILLIAM BRADLEY5, WILLIAM M.4, JACOB3, DANIEL2*

*KRIDER, JOHN MICHAEL*1 *KREIDER)* was born July 14, 1938, in Maryville, Blount Co., Tennessee.

❤ James married L. A. RHODES. She was born April 27,1939.

Children of JAMES KING and L.A. RHODES are:

      i.   DAVID RHODES9 KING, b. October 22, 1962.
     ii.   TANYA DAWN KING, b. September 18, 1967.

159. MARCIA A.8 KING *(MARTHA VIRGINIA*7 *CRIDER, LAWRENCE EDWIN*6*, WILLIAM BRADLEY*5*, WILLIAM M.*4*, JACOB*3*, DANIEL*2 *KRIDER, JOHN MICHAEL*1 *KREIDER)* was born January 6, 1944, in Maryville, Blount Co., Tennessee.

❤ Marcia married G. W. REICHARD Bef. 1968. G.W. was born Nov. 21, 1943.

Children of MARCIA KING and G.W. REICHARD are:

      i.   JENNIFER D.9 REICHARD, b. April 3, 1968.
     ii.   JAMES JEFFREY REICHARD, b. October 16, 1969.

160. SUSAN THERESE8 BOYD *(EMMOGENE CRIDER*7 *JONES, EMMOGENE ANITA*6 *CRIDER, JAMES WINSLOW*5*, THOMAS BENNETT*4*, GEORGE*3*, DANIEL*2 *KRIDER, JOHN MICHAEL*1 *KREIDER)* was born September 11, 1958, in Richmond, Henrico Co., Virginia.

♥ Susan married CLYDE NEAL GAULDIN October 25, 1985, in Richmond, Henrico Co., Virginia.

Child of SUSAN BOYD and CLYDE GAULDIN is:

    i.   GENNA RENE9 GAULDIN, b. June 16, 1986, Richmond, Henrico Co., Virginia.

161. JAY HERBERT8 KRIEGEL *(GLORIA MAY7 JONES, EMMOGENE ANITA6 CRIDER, JAMES WINSLOW5, THOMAS BENNETT4, GEORGE3, DANIEL2 KRIDER, JOHN MICHAEL1 KREIDER)* was born April 28, 1958 in Corydon, Harrison Co., Indiana.

Jay graduated from Newberry College, Newberry, South Carolina in May of 1980 with a B.S. in Business Administration.

♥ Jay married JULIE ANN MULROONEY July 18, 1981, in Doraville, DeKalb Co., Georgia. Julie was born Nov. 17, 1959.

Julie is the daughter of William Robert Mulrooney and Patricia Ann Butler Mulrooney.

Children of JAY KRIEGEL and JULIE MULROONEY are:

    i.   JASON WILLIAM9 KRIEGEL, b. April 3, 1986, Snellville, Gwinnett Co., Georgia.
    ii. JENNA KATHERINE KRIEGEL, b. October 28, 1988, Carrollton, Denton Co., Texas.

162. REBECCA LYNN (SMITH)8 BLACKWELL *(CHRISTINE JOYCE7 JONES, EMMOGENE ANITA6 CRIDER, JAMES WINSLOW5, THOMAS*

*BENNETT*4, *GEORGE*3, *DANIEL*2 *KRIDER, JOHN MICHAEL*1 *KREIDER)*
was born July 21, 1952, in Corinth, Alcorn Co., Mississippi.

Rebecca, being young and not fond the surname Smith, adopted her
great-grandmother's surname, Blackwell, in 1977. In her research she
has since discovered the Smith family originally carried the surname
Arrowsmith, abbreviating it in the early 1800s.

Rebecca graduated from the University of South Florida in 1973 with a
degree in Psychology and went on to graduate work at the Universities
of Virginia and Washington.

She has been a special education teacher since 1976, and she is
currently teaching in Maryland.

Child of REBECCA BLACKWELL:

i. TYLER WEBB9 BLACKWELL, b. April 21, 1993, Washington,
    D.C..

    Tyler is the beloved natural son of Rebecca Blackwell.
    Although his father welcomed him into the world, he is not
    part of Tyler's daily life. Rebecca's family anticipated his birth
    with much joy and love.

    Tyler was born eight weeks early; he weighed 4 lb. 5 oz. and
    was 15 1/2" tall. His aunt Holly Smith attended his caesarian
    birth at George Washington University Hospital in
    Washington, D.C. He spent 20 days in the Intensive Care
    Nursery before going home.

    Tyler's middle name is in honor of his sixth great-grandfather
    on the Smith line, John Webb, who served as a Lt. Colonel in
    Washington's army during the Revolutionary War. It is hoped
    Tyler will inherit his family's interest in history.

163. CLAY BLACKWELL8 SMITH *(CHRISTINE JOYCE7 JONES,*
EMMOGENE ANITA6 CRIDER, JAMES WINSLOW5, THOMAS BENNETT4,
GEORGE3, DANIEL2 KRIDER, JOHN MICHAEL1 KREIDER) was born
February 25, 1956, in Ft. Bragg, Cumberland Co., North Carolina.

Like his Crider ancestors, Clay has labored as a blacksmith. He was
employed by the Colonial Williamsburg Foundation as a blacksmith in
the Anderson Forge for a period of two years. He is now a Journeyman
gunsmith in Colonial Williamsburg, which requires him to continuing
using his blacksmithing skills (1997). His other jobs have included
teaching Native American crafts to Native Americans on four
reservations in Virginia.

♥   Clay married VARA HOLLAND BOTTOMS in January, 1977, in
Richmond, Henrico Co., Virginia, daughter of WILLIAM BOTTOMS and
VARA HOLLAND. Holly was born Mar. 31, 1958, in Richmond,
Henrico Co., Virginia.

Vara Holland Bottoms goes by the name "Holly". After spending
several years as a Neonatal Intensive Care Nurse at the Medical
College of Virginia, Holly became a computer programmer in 1996.

Children of CLAY SMITH and VARA BOTTOMS are:

167.   i.   JESSICA HOLLAND9 SMITH
         ii.   JEREMIAH BLACKWELL SMITH, b. August 21, 1985,
                Richmond, Henrico Co., Virginia.

164. DONNA LYNN8 GRAY *(JESSE ANNA7 JONES, EMMOGENE ANITA6*
CRIDER, JAMES WINSLOW5, THOMAS BENNETT4, GEORGE3, DANIEL2
KRIDER, JOHN MICHAEL1 KREIDER) was born August 1, 1961, in
Corinth, Alcorn Co., Mississippi.

♥ Donna married TONY ALLEN HUGHES June 26, 1983, in Corinth, Alcorn Co., Mississippi. Tony was born Oct. 16, 1957, in Corinth, Alcorn Co, Mississippi.

Tony is the son of William Lonnie Hughes and Gladys Earline Hudson Hughes.

Children of DONNA GRAY and TONY HUGHES are:

> i.   CODY ALLEN9 HUGHES, b. December 6, 1983, Selmer, McNairy Co., Tennessee.
> ii. JUSTIN KYLE HUGHES, b. March 25, 1987, Selmer, McNairy Co., Tennessee.

165. CONSTANCE JUANITA8 JONES *(CHARLOTTE MARIE7, EMMOGENE ANITA6 CRIDER, JAMES WINSLOW5, THOMAS BENNETT4, GEORGE3, DANIEL2 KRIDER, JOHN MICHAEL1 KREIDER)* was born January 24, 1961, in Corinth, Alcorn Co., Mississippi.

♥ Connie married JIMMY RAY REED September 15, 1976, in Corinth, Alcorn Co., Mississippi. Jimmy was born Feb. 17, 1958, in Booneville, Prentiss Co., Mississippi.

Children of CONSTANCE JONES and JIMMY REED are:

> i.   JIMMY RAY9 REED , JR., b. July 7, 1977, Corinth, Alcorn Co., Mississippi.
> ii. JOHN MICHAEL REED, b. November 27, 1979, Corinth, Alcorn Co., Mississippi.
> iii. VALERIE ANN REED, b. September 8, 1982, Corinth, Alcorn Co., Mississippi.

166. HENRIETTA GENE8 CAMPBELL *(HENRY ANANIAS7, ADA FLORENCE6 CRIDER, PRESTON COLUMBUS5, DANIEL BENNETT4, GEORGE3, DANIEL2 KRIDER, JOHN MICHAEL1 KREIDER)* was born June 11, 1929, in Lansing, Ingham Co., Michigan.

♥ Henrietta married (1) HARRY AUERBACH June 24, 1950, in Albuquerque, Bernalillo Co., New Mexico.

Children of HENRIETTA CAMPBELL and HARRY AUERBACH are:

    i.   UNISMARIE H.9 AUERBACH, b. June 8, 1951, Albuquerque, Bernalillo Co., New Mexico.

   ii.   HENDRE JOANN AUERBACH, b. August 5, 1953, Albuquerque, Bernalillo Co., New Mexico.

♥ Henrietta married (2) CHARLES PAUL EDWARDS , SR. April 21, 1966 in Albuquerque, Bernalillo Co., New Mexico.

Children of HENRIETTA CAMPBELL and CHARLES EDWARDS are:

   iii.   RANDALL LEE9 EDWARDS, b. May 21, 1952, Albuquerque, Bernalillo Co., New Mexico.

   iv.   LAURA LOUISE EDWARDS, b. December 9, 1957, Albuquerque, Bernalillo Co., New Mexico.

   v.   LINDA CARROLL EDWARDS, b. August 16, 1959, Albuquerque, Bernalillo Co., New Mexico.

NINTH GENERATION

167. JESSICA HOLLAND9 SMITH(CLAY BLACKWELL8 SMITH, CHRISTINE
JOYCE7 JONES, EMMOGENE ANITA6 CRIDER, JAMES WINSLOW5,
THOMAS BENNETT4, GEORGE3, DANIEL2, JOHN MICHAEL KREIDER1)
was born August 8, 1977, in Richmond, Henrico Co., Virginia.

♥ Jessica married CHRISTOPHER WOOD September 26, 1996, at
Millington, Shelby Co., Tennessee. Chris was born July 14, 1969, at
Ft. Gordon, Stevens Co., Georgia. His parents are James David Wood
and Vera Vaughn.

Child of JESSICA SMITH and CHRIS WOOD is:

     i.   WILLIAM BLACKWELL WOOD, b. March 26, 1997, in
          Memphis, Shelby Co., Tennessee.

INDEX

Entries in all capitals are birth/death and/or marriage records. All other entries are anecdotal.

C

D

H

M

N

O

P

www.ingramcontent.com/pod-product-compliance
Lightning Source LLC
Chambersburg PA
CBHW072235270326

41930CB00010B/2144